Fluency

Grades 4-6

		PAGE
Introduction		i–v

Lessons
Lesson 1a	Read Informational Text with Understanding, Intonation, and Expression	2
Lesson 1b	Read Informational Text with Accuracy, Appropriate Rate, and Expression	4
Lesson 1c	Read Informational Text to Confirm Word Recognition and Understanding	6
Lesson 2a	Read Literary Text with Understanding, Intonation, and Expression	8
Lesson 2b	Read Literary Text with Accuracy, Appropriate Rate, and Expression	10
Lesson 2c	Read Literary Text to Confirm Word Recognition and Understanding	12
Lesson 3a	Read Poetry with Understanding, Intonation, and Expression	14
Lesson 3b	Read Poetry with Accuracy, Appropriate Rate, and Expression	16
Lesson 3c	Read Poetry to Confirm Word Recognition and Understanding	18
Lesson 4a	Read Drama with Understanding, Intonation, and Expression	20
Lesson 4b	Read Drama with Accuracy, Appropriate Rate, and Expression	22
Lesson 4c	Read Drama to Confirm Word Recognition and Understanding	24

Levels D–F Passages with BLMs
BLM 1	Sea Shell: Read for Understanding	26
BLM 2	Sea Shell: Read for Expression	27
BLM 3	Sea Shell: Recognize Words	28
BLM 4	Old Mr. Bear: Read for Understanding	29
BLM 5	Old Mr. Bear: Read for Expression	30
BLM 6	Old Mr. Bear: Recognize Words	31
BLM 7	Pluto: Read for Understanding	32
BLM 8	Pluto: Read for Expression	33
BLM 9	Pluto: Recognize Words	34
BLM 10	A Family of Squirrels: Read for Understanding	35
BLM 11	A Family of Squirrels: Read for Expression	36
BLM 12	A Family of Squirrels: Recognize Words	37

Levels G–I Passages with BLMs
BLM 13	My Shadow: Read for Understanding	38
BLM 14	My Shadow: Read for Expression	39
BLM 15	My Shadow: Recognize Words	40
BLM 16	The Park Pond: Read for Understanding	41
BLM 17	The Park Pond: Read for Expression	42
BLM 18	The Park Pond: Recognize Words	43
BLM 19	Jonas Salk: Read for Understanding	44

BLM 20	Jonas Salk: Read for Expression	45
BLM 21	Jonas Salk: Recognize Words	46
BLM 22	Winston Churchill: Read for Understanding	47
BLM 23	Winston Churchill: Read for Expression	48
BLM 24	Winston Churchill: Recognize Words	49

Levels J–K Passages with BLMs

BLM 25	Bed in Summer: Read for Understanding	50
BLM 26	Bed in Summer: Read for Expression	51
BLM 27	Bed in Summer: Recognize Words	52
BLM 28	The Car Wash: Read for Understanding	53
BLM 29	The Car Wash: Read for Expression	54
BLM 30	The Car Wash: Recognize Words	55
BLM 31	Geno's Insects: Read for Understanding	56
BLM 32	Geno's Insects: Read for Expression	57
BLM 33	Geno's Insects: Recognize Words	58
BLM 34	Smiley the Crocodile: Read for Understanding	59
BLM 35	Smiley the Crocodile: Read for Expression	60
BLM 36	Smiley the Crocodile: Recognize Words	61

Levels L–M Passages with BLMs

BLM 37	The Wind and the Moon: Read for Understanding	62
BLM 38	The Wind and the Moon: Read for Expression	63
BLM 39	The Wind and the Moon: Recognize Words	64
BLM 40	PJ the Parrot: Read for Understanding	65
BLM 41	PJ the Parrot: Read for Expression	66
BLM 42	PJ the Parrot: Recognize Words	67
BLM 43	Body Movement: Read for Understanding	68
BLM 44	Body Movement: Read for Expression	69
BLM 45	Body Movement: Recognize Words	70
BLM 46	The Importance of Strong Leadership: Read for Understanding	71
BLM 47	The Importance of Strong Leadership: Read for Expression	72
BLM 48	The Importance of Strong Leadership: Recognize Words	73

Level N Passages with BLMs

BLM 49	The Planting of the Apple-Tree: Read for Understanding	74
BLM 50	The Planting of the Apple-Tree: Read for Expression	75
BLM 51	The Planting of the Apple-Tree: Recognize Words	76
BLM 52	The Dog Walkers: Read for Understanding	77
BLM 53	The Dog Walkers: Read for Expression	78
BLM 54	The Dog Walkers: Recognize Words	79
BLM 55	Plant Genetics: Read for Understanding	80
BLM 56	Plant Genetics: Read for Expression	81
BLM 57	Plant Genetics: Recognize Words	82
BLM 58	Pyramids to Skyscrapers: Read for Understanding	83
BLM 59	Pyramids to Skyscrapers: Read for Expression	84
BLM 60	Pyramids to Skyscrapers: Recognize Words	85

BLM 61	Recording Time Sheet	86
BLM 62	Comprehension Monitoring	87
BLM 63	Self-Evaluation	88

About *Benchmark Advance* Intervention

Benchmark Advance Intervention is intended for students who need extra support to master grade-level standards. It offers reteaching and additional practice to reinforce instruction in the core program. *Benchmark Advance* Intervention provides direct instruction of the Reading Standards for Foundational Skills, Grades K–5, as outlined in the Common Core State Standards. The standards are addressed as shown below.

Grade **K**	Grade **1**	Grade **2**	Grade **3**	Grades **4–6**
Print Concepts	**Print Concepts**	**Print Concepts**	**Print Concepts**	**Phonics and Word Recognition**
Phonological Awareness	**Phonological Awareness**	**Phonological Awareness**	**Phonological Awareness**	**Fluency**
Phonics and Word Recognition	**Phonics and Word Recognition**	**Phonics and Word Recognition**	**Phonics and Word Recognition**	
Fluency	**Fluency**	**Fluency**	**Fluency**	

At Grades K–3, individual grade-level packages of lessons and blackline masters address all of the Reading Foundation (RF) standards. An additional package for Grades 4–6 addresses the Phonics and Word Recognition and Fluency standards for Grades 2–5. In addition, each of the packages at K-3 includes lessons and blackline masters to address the RF standards presented in previous grades. In this way, teachers can address the needs of students at each student's instructional-level—whether at/near grade level or below.

The program offers skill-focused sequential and systematic instruction that is parallel to instruction in the core program. Each lesson is designed to target a specific skill that needs bolstering as revealed through program assessments.

It can be implemented flexibly in small groups or to individual students. Each lesson is designed to be completed in 15 minutes.

Lesson Structure

All of the fluency lessons in *Benchmark Advance* Intervention follow a consistent instructional design that offers explicit skills instruction and a gradual release model to scaffold student learning.

The side column at the start of every lesson furnishes the information teachers need to manage student learning.

- The target standard or standards appear at the beginning of each lesson.
- The prerequisite lesson(s) that should be completed before using the current lesson are listed.
- The specific Lesson Objective states what students will be able to do after completing the lesson.
- The Essential Question helps bring focus to the standard that is the focus of the lesson.
- The Metacognitive Strategy increases awareness of the strategies students use as they learn.
- The essential academic language and Additional Materials that students will use in the lesson are listed.
- Every lesson offers a reminder of the pre-requisite skills that students need to fully understand the lesson.

The instructional lessons offer consistent and explicit instruction that helps students focus on the specific lesson objectives.

- The Introduce and State Learning Goal sections set the learning goal for the lesson.
- The Before Read-Aloud or Before Reading section offers the opportunity to build background, activate prior knowledge, and make predictions.
- The During Read-Aloud or During Reading section includes teacher modeling, interactive reading, and echo-reading to build intonation and expression.
- The After Read-Aloud or After Reading section includes model questions for students to ask and answer and retelling options to check comprehension.
- The Conclusion gives students an opportunity to restate what they've learned in the lesson.
- The Home Connection links the lesson to at-home practice within the family setting.

Every lesson ends with a point-of-use formative assessment so teachers can evaluate whether students have mastered the target skills. Intervention 2 suggestions provide alternative teaching ideas for working with students who need further support.

The blackline masters that accompany the lessons provide practice and application opportunities to promote standards mastery.

Corrective Feedback

Inherent in the teaching profession is the need to make corrections. In both structural and communicative approaches to language teaching and learning, feedback is viewed as a means of fostering learner motivation and ensuring linguistic accuracy (Ellis 2009). The purpose of the feedback is to close the gap between the student's current learning status and the lesson goals (Sadler 1989). Students can receive feedback in three ways: from their teachers, from peers, and through self-assessment.

Formative assessment is a process that teachers and students use during instruction. It provides feedback to inform ongoing teaching and learning approaches. Corrective feedback is also an essential feature of language development instruction. Teachers provide students with judiciously selected corrective feedback on language usage in ways that are transparent and meaningful to students. Overcorrection or arbitrary corrective feedback is avoided.

Corrective feedback is information given to learners regarding a linguistic error they have made (Loewen 2012; Sheen 2007). The feedback information can consist of any one or all of the following:

  (a) **an indication that an error has been committed,**

  (b) **provision of the correct target language form, or**

  (c) **metalinguistic information about the nature of the error.**

Corrective feedback in the form of negotiating for meaning can help learners notice their errors and create meaningful connections, thus aiding acquisition. It is important to emphasize that language learners can only self-correct if they possess the necessary linguistic knowledge (Ellis 2003).

One solution sometimes advocated to this problem is to conduct corrective feedback as a two-stage process: first encourage self-correction and then, if that fails, provide the correction (Doughty and Varela, 1998).

Corrective feedback can be:

Explicit
Explicit corrective feedback overtly draws the learner's attention to the error made.

Implicit
Implicit corrective feedback focuses the learner's attention without overtly informing the learner that he/she has made an error or interrupting the flow of interaction.

Corrective Feedback Strategies

	IMPLICIT Attracts learner's attention without overtly informing the learner that he/she has made an error or interrupting the flow of interaction.	EXPLICIT Tries to overtly draw the learner's attention to the error made.
INPUT PROVIDING: **Correct form is given to students.**	**RECAST** The teacher incorporates the content words of the immediately preceding incorrect utterance and changes and corrects the utterance in some way (e.g., phonological, syntactic, morphological, or lexical). L: I went school. T: You went to school?	**EXPLICIT CORRECTION** The teacher indicates an error has been committed, identifies the error, and provides the correction. L: We will go on May. T: Not *on* May, *in* May. T: We will go in May.
OUTPUT PROMPTING: **The student is prompted to self-correct.**	**REPETITION** The teacher repeats the learner utterance highlighting the error by means of emphatic stress. L: I will showed you. T: I will *show* you. L: I will show you.	**METALINGUISTIC EXPLANATION** The teacher provides explanation for the errors that have been made. L: two duck T: Do you remember how to show more than one duck? L: ducks T: Yes, you remember that we need to add "s" at the end of a noun to show the plural form.
	CLARIFICATION REQUEST The corrector indicates that he/she has not understood what the learner said. L: on the it go T: Can you please tell me again? T: Do you mean "it goes on your desk"?	**ELICITATION** The teacher repeats part of the learner utterance, but not the erroneous part, and uses rising intonation to signal the learner should complete it. L: I don't think won't rain. T: I don't think it…(will) rain.
		PARALINGUISTIC SIGNAL The teacher uses a gesture or facial expression to indicate that the learner has made an error. L: Yesterday I go to the movies. T: (gestures with right forefinger over left shoulder to indicate past)

Adapted from: Ellis, Rod. "Corrective Feedback and Teacher Development." L2 Journal, volume 1, (2009).

Recommendations for English Learners

	Student Language and Literacy Characteristics	Considerations for Instructions
Oral Skills	**No or little spoken English proficiency**	**Students will need instruction in recognizing and distinguishing the sounds of English as compared or contrasted with sounds in their native language.** • The Center for the Improvement of Early Reading Achievement (CIERA) states that English learners should learn to read initially in their first language. CIERA recommends that English learners participate in read-alouds of big books, read along with proficient readers, and listen repeatedly to books read aloud in order to gain fluency in English (Hiebert et al., 1998). • Rhymes, poems, stories and songs are present in most languages and cultures. The act of repeated listening to rhymes, poems, stories, and songs will help students become familiar and internalize the sounds and rhythm of the English language. • The particular language of rhymes, poems, stories, and songs will encourage and motivate English learners to begin to produce both the familiar and unfamiliar sounds of the English language. • Use Visuals, gestures, emphasized rhythm and varied voice intonation are used to convey and negotiate meaning.
	Oral skills: Spoken English proficiency	**Students will need instruction in applying their knowledge of the English sound system to foundational literacy learning.** • Rhymes, poems, stories and songs provide English learners the opportunity to practice and build on the English language they already know. • The repetitive and playful language in rhymes, poems, and songs motivates English learners and helps them to feel confident and successful as they produce English fluently, with intonation and expression.
Print Skills	**No or little native language literacy**	**Students will need instruction in print concepts.** • Fluency practice includes basic print concepts such as tracking from left to right, return sweep, top to bottom, and page-by-page sequence. It also includes recognizing and naming all upper- and lowercase letters of the alphabet and understanding that letters represent sounds and, most important, that print carries a message.
	Some foundational literacy proficiency in a language not using the Latin alphabet (e.g., Arabic, Chinese, Korean, Russian)	**Students will be familiar with print concepts, and will need instruction in learning the Latin alphabet for English, as compared or contrasted with their native language writing system (e.g., direction of print, symbols representing whole words, syllables, or phonemes).** • Beyond the directionality of print, and the relationship between phonemes and graphemes, engaging in meaningful repeated readings will help English learners gain familiarity with the Latin alphabet and the sounds it represents as well as building their foundational proficiency in English reading comprehension. • Using visuals, gestures, emphasized rhythm, and varied voice intonation and relating those specifically to words and phrases in the text will underscore that print, whether logographic or alphabetic, is the expression of thought and carries a message that can be voiced.
	Some foundational literacy proficiency in a language using the Latin alphabet (e.g., Spanish)	**Students will need instruction in applying their knowledge of print concepts, phonics, and word recognition to the English writing system, as compared or contrasted with their native language alphabet (e.g., letters that are the same or different, or represent the same or different sounds) and native language vocabulary (e.g., cognates) and sentence structure (e.g., subject-verb-object vs. subject-object-verb word order).** • Familiarity with the Latin alphabet affords students the opportunity to avail themselves of their primary language skills to transfer their knowledge to English. • Repeated purposeful readings will enable students to construct meaning as they develop and produce the English language with fluency, intonation, and expression.

Please see the Contrastive Analysis Charts provided in the Teacher's Resource Guide.

Read Informational Text with Understanding, Intonation, and Expression RF.4–5.4a

CCSS: RF.4–5.4
Read with sufficient accuracy and fluency to support comprehension.
a. Read on-level text with purpose and understanding.

Lesson Objectives

- Determine genre of text before reading and demonstrate understanding of the purpose for reading.
- Demonstrate an understanding of grade-appropriate vocabulary.
- Participate in guided/shared reading of different genres of text.
- Make and confirm predictions in text read aloud by the teacher.
- Read with intonation and expression.

Essential Question

How do readers know what kind of expression to use?

Metacognitive Strategy

Think while listening; plan, monitor, and evaluate listening; reference visuals and text features to predict and confirm understanding.

Academic Language

Informational text, topic; facts, details, explain, predict, sequence, first, next, then, last, finally

Additional Materials

- BLMs 7, 10, 19, 22, 43, 46, 55, 58, Read for Understanding
- BLM 63, Self-Evaluation

Pre-Assess

Student's ability to listen with attention, to understand what is read aloud, and to use text features.

Understand how voice and expression are used to convey the meaning of a text read-aloud.

Introduce

- Students will be aware of a specific purpose for listening and reading.
- Students will demonstrate listening comprehension by responding to wh-questions or explaining what the text read-aloud is about.
- Students will demonstrate listening retention by explaining facts and details, using illustrations, text features, and recalling words/phrases from the text.

State Learning Goal

Say: *Today we will read an* **informational text**. *The purpose for listening to the informational text will be to remember what it is about, and to remember facts and details we found interesting. You will first listen to the sound and tone of my voice as it changes when I read aloud.*

Ask: *What is the purpose for listening today? (to remember what the text is about, to listen how the voice changes)*

Before Read-Aloud

Use the title and text features to establish the **topic** and activate prior knowledge. Build background knowledge by discussing text language and key vocabulary to make certain students understand their meaning.

Ask: *What do you* **predict** *this text will be about? (Point out title, text features, and details in illustrations as clues to prediction.)*

During Read-Aloud

First Read: Model reading fluently at a natural pace with intonation and expression, including emphasis on key **facts** or **details**, varying voice intonation to engage students and facilitate comprehension. Model reading without intonation, emphasis, or expression.

Ask: *Which reading did you like best? Why?*

Second Read: Interactive reading while thinking aloud, asking thoughtful questions, emphasizing key details, and confirming predictions.

Have students:

Grade 4

- **Explain** and draw inferences from the text by referring to details and examples in text.
- Determine the main idea of a text and explain how it is supported by key details; summarize text.
- Explain events, procedures, ideas, or concepts in a historical, scientific, or technical text, including what happened and why based on specific information in the text.

Grade 5

- Quote accurately from the text when explaining what the text says explicitly and when drawing inferences.
- Determine two or more main ideas and how they are supported by key details; summarize the text.
- Explain the relationship or interactions between two or more individuals, events, ideas, or concepts in a historical, scientific, or technical text based on specific information in the text.

Grade 6

- Cite textual evidence to support analysis of what the text says explicitly as well as inferences drawn from the text.
- Determine a central idea of a text and explain how it is conveyed through particular details; provide a summary of the text distinct from personal opinions or judgments.
- Analyze in detail how a key individual, event, or idea is introduced, illustrated, and elaborated upon in a text (e.g., through examples and anecdotes).

Third Read: Echo-read or choral-read with students emphasizing appropriate pacing, intonation, and expression.

Say: *When we read aloud, the sound of our voice also gives meaning to the words.*

After Read-Aloud

Have students demonstrate understanding of the text by asking them to retell the text in their own words using key details. Support students by providing sentence starters as needed.

A topic is what the text is mostly about: The topic of this passage is _____.

A detail is information about the topic: One fact or detail the text provides is _____.

Making connections to the text: I learned that _____ is/are/can/ _____ and also that _____.

Conclusion

Ask: *What did we learn today?*

We learned that when we read, our voices and expressions change along with the words. We read as we speak, not too fast and not too slow, so that we can understand what we read.

Use BLM 63 for student self-reflection, evaluation, and goal setting.

Home Connection

Ask students to take the informational text home to reread with a family member. Have students point out key details and events they remember and discuss with their family what the informational text is about.

✓ Formative Assessment
If the student completes each task correctly, proceed to the next skill in the sequence. If not, refer to suggested Intervention 2.

Did the student…?	Intervention 2
Recall the purpose for listening?	• Explain that a "purpose" is a "reason." Explain that we pay attention to what is read with a purpose. • **Say:** *We will listen to remember what the informational text is about. We will remember key details and events.* (Provide examples.)
Connect to prior knowledge?	• Build new knowledge using illustrations and provide personal examples that connect to what students already know.
Build understanding of vocabulary?	• Use visuals, quick sketches, gestures, and realia. Provide definitions and examples.
Predict what the informational text was about?	• Make connections between title, illustrations, and key vocabulary.
Recall key details and events?	• Reference informational text board illustrations, number events to correlate with illustrations. • Use informational text structure graphic organizer to sketch and analyze text elements.
Echo- or choral-read?	• Echo-read one phrase or sentence at a time, and check for understanding.
Retell informational text?	• Use informational text board and sentence frames or sentence starters correlated to each picture.

Read Informational Text with Accuracy, Appropriate Rate, and Expression RF.4–5.4b

CCSS: RF.4–5.4
Read with sufficient accuracy and fluency to support comprehension.
b Read on-level text orally with accuracy, appropriate rate, and expression on successive readings.

Prerequisite lesson
Fluency: Lesson 1a

Lesson Objectives

- Listen to different genres read aloud fluently.
- Read with accuracy, appropriate rate, and expression.
- Decode instructional-level words with increasing automaticity.
- Read sight words accurately and automatically.
- Use phrasing/fluency technique.

Essential Questions

How does grouping words help you read better?
How does punctuation help a reader?

Metacognitive Strategy

Selective attention and monitoring comprehension while reading

Academic Language

Pacing, fluency, words, phrases

Additional Materials

- BLMs 8, 11, 20, 23, 44, 47, 56, 59, Read for Expression
- BLM 63, Self Evaluation

Pre-Assess

Student's ability to decode instructional-level words with automaticity, and understand text while reading it aloud.

Introduce

- Students will be aware of a specific purpose for reading.
- Students will read with proper phrasing and fluency.
- Students will demonstrate automaticity of instructional-level words.

State Learning Goal

Say: *Today we will read an* **informational text***. The purpose for reading the informational text today is to read with appropriate pacing and fluency. That means we will not read too fast or too slow, so that we can understand what we are reading. We will read words and phrases aloud so that we can practice reading and understanding what we read.*

Ask: *What is the purpose for reading today? (I will read words and phrases aloud so I can understand what I read).*

Before Reading

Explain that successful readers know when to pause when reading and how to read words that go together without stopping.

Say: *We are going to read an informational text and practice pausing and reading words that go together naturally.*

During Reading

First Read: Teacher models reading each sentence with proper phrasing and fluency. Teacher reads the whole passage, pointing out punctuation marks and rereading, asking the student to listen to the changes in the tone of voice.

Second Read: Student reads each sentence progressively, scrolling down each line of the text.

Third Read: Student reads the whole informational text with appropriate fluency and pacing. Teacher monitors for student's accuracy, fluency, and pacing.

After Reading

Have students read to partners to demonstrate that they can use the sentence progression strategy to practice appropriate fluency and pacing.

Conclusion

Ask: *What did we learn today?*

We learned how to pause when reading and how to read phrases that go together naturally. We read as we speak, not too fast and not too slow, so that we can understand what we read. Punctuation helps readers know when to pause, stop, and change their tone of voice. Reading with appropriate pacing and intonation helps us understand what we read.

Use BLM 63 for student self-reflection, evaluation, and goal setting.

Home Connection

Ask students to take the informational text home to read with a family member. Have students practice the sentence progression strategy.

✔ Formative Assessment

If the student completes each task correctly, proceed to the next skill in the sequence. If not, refer to suggested Intervention 2.

Did the student…?	Intervention 2
Recall the purpose for reading?	• Explain that a "purpose" is a "reason." Explain that we pay attention to how we read the text aloud so that it sounds like we are talking. This helps us understand what we are reading. • **Say:** *We have to make sure that we are not reading too fast or too slow. We will read each word followed by the next until the words become a sentence.*
Listen attentively while teacher modeled?	• Model reading fluently while students echo- or choral-read. Conduct a cloze read as student chimes in missing words.
Read each sentence progressively?	• Guide students in reading the words, phrases, and sentences by scrolling the text to expose one line at a time while it is being read.
Scroll from one line to another effortlessly?	• Have students practice tracking each word and use the return sweep with their finger as you read aloud together.
Read informational text with appropriate pacing?	• Guide students by tracking across the line of text while reading aloud together.
Read informational text with appropriate intonation?	• Select a portion of the text that requires varied intonation. Discuss the meaning, feelings, and thoughts conveyed by the text to explain why changing the tone of voice is necessary to express meaning and understand the text.

CCSS: RF.4–5.4
Read with sufficient accuracy and fluency to support comprehension.
c. Use context to confirm or self-correct word recognition and understanding, rereading as necessary.

Prerequisite lessons
Fluency: Lessons 1a and 1b

Lesson Objectives

- Read with purpose and understanding, determining if the text is not understood.
- Read with accuracy and comprehension, determining if a word is misread.
- Use context to determine meaning.
- Decode instructional-level words with increasing automaticity.

Essential Questions

What do I do when I do not know what a word means?
What is an appropriate rate in reading?

Metacognitive Strategy

Use selective attention and monitor comprehension; make inferences and use context clues.

Academic Language

Accuracy, comprehension

Additional Materials

- BLMs 9, 12, 21, 24, 45, 48, 57, 60, Recognize Words
- BLM 61, Recording Time Sheet
- BLM 62, Comprehension Monitoring
- BLM 63, Self Evaluation

Pre-Assess

Student's ability to decode instructional-level words with automaticity, and understand text while reading it aloud.

Read Informational Text to Confirm Word Recognition and Understanding RF.4–5.4c

Introduce

- Students will be aware of a specific purpose for reading.

- Students will read with accuracy and understanding, determining when they do not understand word or text meaning.

- Students will demonstrate automaticity of instructional-level words.

State Learning Goal

Say: *Today we will read an* **informational text***. The purpose for reading the text today is to read with accuracy and understanding. That means we will practice reading every word correctly and understand what each word means. We will be aware when we do not understand the meaning of what we read or are confused by a word or phrase.*

Ask: *What is the purpose for reading today? (I will read correctly (with accuracy) and know what each word means).*

Before Reading

Explain that successful readers are able to read and understand what they read. When they do not understand what they are reading, they stop and reread. They think about what they have read and determine meaning before continuing. If they cannot figure out the meaning of a word, they look for clues such as the words around the word they do not know and word parts that may provide a clue to the meaning of the word they do not know.

Say: *We are going to practice reading each word correctly, making sure we understand the meaning of each word.*

Read the list of words and have students identify words they do not know. Use context clues to explain the meaning of unknown words. Redefine words as needed. Example:

Unknown Word	Word in Context	Word Redefined
(student-generated)	as it appears in sentence	Look at word parts (structural clues). Look up in dictionary (definition). Look at surrounding words (context clues). Determine if it is a cognate.

During Reading

First Read: Teacher models rereading words correctly and fluently.

Second Read: Teacher uses the Recording Time Sheet BLM (61) to monitor first fluency and accuracy rate.

Student reads each word on list. Teacher identifies and annotates student's errors and self-corrections, and discusses word/phrase relationship to overall passage (multiple meanings, synonyms/antonyms, roots, affixes).

Third Read: Student reads the whole passage aloud to self or to a partner with appropriate fluency and pacing, recording the second fluency and **accuracy** rate.

After Reading

Use the Comprehension Monitoring BLM (62) to monitor and record comprehension. Ask text-dependent questions to ensure student understanding. Ask students to retell or explain text in their own words to check for **comprehension**.

- What is this text about?
- Recall two important facts or details you remember about _____. 1) _____ 2) _____
- Explain in your own words what the author is saying about _____.
- What idea does the author present first?
- What does he/she tell us next?
- Why is this information important? Cite text evidence.
- Which piece of information is the most important? Cite text evidence.
- What have you learned from reading this text?
- How does _____ relate to _____?
- How does this text conclude?

Conclusion

Ask: *What did we learn today?*

We learned to read words correctly and understand what we read. When we read, it is important to read the words correctly and understand the meaning of the words we read.

Use BLM 63 for student self-reflection, evaluation, and goal setting.

Home Connection

Send home a copy of the text and the Recording Time Sheet BLM. Have a family member time and record the student's reading.

✔ Formative Assessment

If the student completes each task correctly, proceed to the next skill in the sequence. If not, refer to suggested Intervention 2.

Did the student…?	Intervention 2
Recall the purpose for reading?	• Explain that a "purpose" is a "reason." Explain that we pay attention to how we read the text aloud so that it sounds like we are talking. This helps us understand what we are reading. • **Say:** *We have to make sure that we are not reading too fast or too slow. We will read each word followed by the next until the words become a sentence.*
Listen attentively while teacher modeled?	• Model reading fluently while students echo- or choral-read. Conduct a cloze read as students chime in missing words.
Read each sentence progressively?	• Guide students in reading the words, phrases, and sentences by scrolling the text to expose one line at a time while it is being read.
Scroll from one line to another effortlessly?	• Have students practice tracking each word and use the return sweep with their finger as you read aloud together.
Read informational text with appropriate pacing?	• Practice reading the word list and match words from the list to the text.
Read informational text with appropriate intonation?	• Select a portion of the text that requires varied intonation. Discuss the meaning, feelings, and the thoughts conveyed by the text to explain why changing the tone of voice is necessary to express meaning and understand the text.

Read Literary Text with Understanding, Intonation, and Expression RF.4–5.4a

CCSS: RF.4–5.4
Read with sufficient accuracy and fluency to support comprehension.
a. Read on-level grade text with purpose and understanding.

Lesson Objectives

- Determine genre of text before reading and demonstrate understanding of the purpose for reading.
- Demonstrate an understanding of grade-appropriate vocabulary.
- Participate in guided/shared reading of different genres of text.
- Make and confirm predictions in text read-aloud by the teacher.
- Read with intonation and expression.

Essential Question

How do readers know what kind of expression to use?

Metacognitive Strategy

Think while listening; plan, monitor, and evaluate listening; reference pictures/visuals/illustrations to predict and confirm understanding.

Academic Language

Story, character, setting, events, details, retell, predict, sequence, first, next, then, last, finally

Additional Materials

- BLMs 4, 16, 28, 31, 34, 40, 52, 63 Read for Understanding
- BLM 63, Self Evaluation

Pre-Assess

Student's ability to listen with attention, understand what is read aloud, and use picture clues.

Understand how voice and expression are used to convey the meaning of a text read-aloud.

Introduce

- Students will be aware of a specific purpose for listening and reading.
- Students will demonstrate listening comprehension by responding to wh-questions or explaining what the text read-aloud is about.
- Students will demonstrate listening retention by retelling and recalling words/phrases from the text.

State Learning Goal

Say: *Today we will read a* **story**. *The purpose for listening to the story will be to remember what the story is about, and to remember sequence of events and details we enjoyed. Listen to the sound and tone of my voice as it changes when I read aloud.*

Ask: *What is the purpose for listening today? (to remember what the story is about, to listen to voice changes)*

Before Read-Aloud

Use the title and illustrations to establish the main idea/theme and activate prior knowledge. Build background knowledge by discussing text language and key vocabulary to make certain students understand their meaning.

Ask: *What do you* **predict** *this story will be about? (Point out title and details in illustrations as clues to prediction.)*

During Read-Aloud

First Read: Model reading fluently at a natural pace with intonation, rhythm, and expression. Include dramatic gestures and varied voice intonation of dialogue to engage students and facilitate comprehension. Model reading without intonation, rhythm, and expression.

Ask: *Which reading did you like best? Why?*

Second Read: Interactive reading while thinking aloud, asking thoughtful questions, emphasizing key details, and confirming predictions.

Have students:

Grade 4

- Explain and draw inferences about what the text says by referring to details and examples.
- Determine theme of the story through details in the story—summarize.
- Describe in depth the characters, setting, and events using text evidence.

Grade 5

- Quote accurately from the text when explaining what the text says explicitly and when drawing inferences.
- Determine a theme of the story from details in text including how characters respond to challenges.
- Compare and contrast two or more **characters, settings,** and **events**—using text evidence.

Grade 6

- Cite textual evidence to support analysis of what the text says explicitly, as well as inference using evidence.
- Determine the theme or central idea of the text and how it is conveyed through specific details; provide a summary without including personal opinions and judgments.
- Describe how a particular story's plot unfolds in a series of episodes.
- Describe how characters respond or change as the plot moves towards resolution.

Third Read: Echo-read or choral-read with students, emphasizing appropriate pacing, intonation, and expression.

Say: *When we read, the sound of our voice gives meaning to the words.*

After Read-Aloud

Have students demonstrate understanding of the text by asking them to retell the story in their own words using key details. Support students by providing question prompts for a sequence of events such as: *What happened first? Next? Then? Last?*

Conclusion

Ask: *What did we learn today?*

We learned that when we read, our voices and expression change along with the words. We read as we speak, not too fast and not too slow, so that we can understand what we read.

Use BLM 63 for student self-reflection, evaluation, and goal setting.

Home Connection

Ask students to take the story home to reread with a family member. Have students point out key details and events they remember and discuss with their family what the story is about.

✔ Formative Assessment

If the student completes each task correctly, proceed to the next skill in the sequence. If not, refer to suggested Intervention 2.

Did the student…?	Intervention 2
Recall the purpose for listening?	• Explain that a "purpose" is a "reason." Explain that we pay attention to what is read with a purpose. Say: We will listen to remember what the story is about. Say: We will remember key details and events. (Provide examples.)
Connect to prior knowledge?	• Build new knowledge using illustrations and provide personal examples that connect to what students already know.
Build understanding of vocabulary?	• Use visuals, quick sketches, gestures, and realia. Provide definitions and examples.
Predict what story was about?	• Make connections between title, illustrations, and key vocabulary.
Recall key details and events?	• Use a story structure graphic organizer to sketch and analyze story elements.
Echo- or choral-read?	• Echo-read one phrase or sentence at a time, and check for understanding.
Retell story?	• Use a story structure graphic organizer to help students recall and retell the story.

CCSS: RF.4–5.4
Read with sufficient accuracy and fluency to support comprehension.
b. Read on-level text orally with accuracy, appropriate rate, and expression on successive readings.

Prerequisite lesson

Fluency: Lesson 2a

Lesson Objectives

- Listen to different genres read aloud fluently.
- Read with accuracy, appropriate rate, and expression.
- Decode instructional-level words with increasing automaticity.
- Read sight words accurately and automatically.
- Use phrasing/fluency technique.

Essential Questions

How does grouping words help you read better?
How does punctuation help a reader?

Metacognitive Strategy

Use selective attention and monitor comprehension while reading.

Academic Language

Pacing, fluency, words, phrases

Additional Materials

- BLMs 5, 17, 29, 32, 35, 41, 53, Read for Expression
- BLM 63, Self-Evaluation

Pre-Assess

Student's ability to decode instructional-level words with automaticity, and understand text while reading it aloud.

Read Literary Text with Accuracy, Appropriate Rate, and Expression RF.4–5.4b

Introduce

- Students will be aware of a specific purpose for reading.
- Students will read with proper phrasing and fluency.
- Students will demonstrate automaticity of instructional-level words.

State Learning Goal

Say: *Today we will read a* **story**. *The purpose for reading the story today is to read with appropriate pacing and fluency. That means we will not read too fast or too slow, so that we can understand what we are reading. We will read words and phrases aloud so we can practice reading and understanding what we read.*

Ask: *What is the purpose for reading today? (I will read words and phrases aloud so I can understand what I read.)*

Before Reading

Explain that successful readers know when to pause when reading and how to read words that go together without stopping.

Say: *We are going to read the story and practice pausing and reading words that go together naturally.*

During Reading

First Read: Teacher models reading each sentence with proper phrasing and **fluency**. Teacher reads the whole passage, pointing out punctuation marks and rereading, asking the student to listen to the changes in the tone of voice.

Second Read: Student reads each sentence progressively, scrolling down each line of the story.

Third Read: Student reads the whole story with appropriate fluency and pacing. Teacher monitors for student's accuracy, fluency, and pacing.

After Reading

Have students read to partners to demonstrate that they can use the sentence progression strategy to practice appropriate fluency and **pacing**.

Conclusion

Ask: *What did we learn today?*

We learned how to pause when reading and how to read phrases that go together naturally. We read as we speak, not too fast and not too slow, so that we can understand what we read. Punctuation helps readers know when to pause, stop, and change their tone of voice. Reading with appropriate pacing and intonation helps us understand what we read.

Use BLM 63 for student self-reflection, evaluation, and goal setting.

Home Connection

Ask students to take the story home to read with a family member. Have students practice the sentence progression strategy with family members.

✔ Formative Assessment

If the student completes each task correctly, proceed to the next skill in the sequence. If not, refer to suggested Intervention 2.

Did the student…?	Intervention 2
Recall the purpose for reading?	• Explain that a "purpose" is a "reason." Explain that we pay attention to how we read the text aloud so that it sounds like we are talking. This helps us understand what we are reading. • **Say:** *We have to make sure that we are not reading too fast or too slow. We will read each word followed by the next until the words become a sentence.*
Listen attentively while teacher modeled?	• Model reading fluently while students echo- or choral-read. Conduct a cloze read as students chime in missing words.
Read each sentence progressively?	• Guide students in reading the words, phrases, and sentences by scrolling the text to expose one line at a time while it is being read.
Scroll from one line to another effortlessly?	• Have students practice tracking each word and use the return sweep with their finger as you read aloud together.
Read story with appropriate pacing?	• Guide students by tracking across the line of text while reading aloud together.
Read story with appropriate intonation?	• Select a portion of the text that requires varied intonation. Discuss the meaning, feelings, and thoughts conveyed by the text to explain why changing the tone of voice is necessary to express meaning and understand the text.

Read Literary Text to Confirm Word Recognition and Understanding RF.4–5.4c

CCSS: RF.4–5.4
Read with sufficient accuracy and fluency to support comprehension.
c. Use context to confirm or self-correct word recognition and understanding, rereading as necessary.

Prerequisite lessons

Fluency: Lessons 2a and 2b

Lesson Objectives

- Read with purpose and understanding, determining if text is not understood.
- Read with accuracy and comprehension, determining if a word is misread.
- Use context to determine meaning.
- Decode instructional-level words with increasing automaticity.

Essential Questions

What do I do when I do not know what a word means?
What is an appropriate rate in reading?

Metacognitive Strategy

Selective attention and monitoring comprehension while reading; Make inferences and use context clues

Academic Language

Accuracy, comprehension

Additional Materials

- BLMs 6, 18, 30, 33, 36, 42, 54, Recognize Words
- BLM 61, Recording Time Sheet
- BLM 62, Monitor Comprehension
- BLM 63, Self-Evaluation

Pre-Assess

Student's ability to decode instructional-level words with automaticity, and understand text while reading it aloud.

Introduce

- Students will be aware of a specific purpose for reading.
- Students will read with accuracy and understanding, determining when they do not understand words or text meaning.
- Students will demonstrate automaticity of instructional-level words.

State Learning Goal

Say: *Today we will read a* **story***. The purpose for reading the story today is to read with accuracy and understanding. That means we will practice reading every word correctly and understand what each word means. We will be aware when we do not understand the meaning of what we read or are confused by a word or phrase. When we do not understand what we read, we will stop to figure it out.*

Ask: *What is the purpose for reading today? (I will read correctly (with accuracy) and know what each word means.).*

Before Reading

Explain that successful readers are able to read and understand what they read. When they do not understand what they are reading, they stop and reread. They think about what they have read and determine meaning before continuing. If they cannot figure out the meaning of a word, they look for clues such as the words around the word they do not know and word parts that may provide a clue to the meaning of the word they do not know.

Say: *We are going to practice reading each word correctly, making sure we understand the meaning of each word.*

Read the list of words and have students identify words they do not know. Use context clues to explain the meaning of unknown words. Redefine words as needed. Example:

Unknown Word	Word in Context	Word Redefined
(student-generated)	as it appears in sentence	Look at word parts (structural clues). Look up in dictionary (definition). Look at surrounding words (context clues). Determine if it is a cognate.

During Reading

First Read: Teacher models reading words correctly and fluently.

Second Read: Teacher uses the Recording Time Sheet BLM (61) to monitor first fluency and accuracy rate.

Student reads each word on list. Teacher identifies and annotates student's errors and self-corrections, and discusses word/phrase relationship to overall passage (multiple meanings, synonyms/antonyms, roots, affixes).

Third Read: Student reads the whole story aloud to self or to a partner with appropriate fluency and pacing, recording the second fluency and accuracy rate.

After Reading

Use the Comprehension Monitoring BLM (62) to monitor and record comprehension. Ask text-dependent questions to ensure student understanding. Ask students to retell or explain text in their own words to check for comprehension.

- In your own words, what is this story about?
- What is the problem in the story? How do you know?
- Who are characters in this story? What are their names?
- Who is the main character? Cite text evidence.
- Compare two characters in the story.
- What is the setting of this story? How do you know?
- What are the characters doing? How are they doing this? Why do you think they are doing this?
- What is the plot of the story? Are there any plot changes? How does the main character respond?
- Can this really happen? Why or why not?
- What happened first, next, then, last?

Conclusion

Ask: *What did we learn today?*

We learned that good readers read words correctly and understand what they read. When we read, it is important to read the words correctly and understand the meaning of the words we read.

Use BLM 63 for student self-reflection, evaluation, and goal setting.

Home Connection

Provide students a copy of the story and the Recording Time Sheet BLM. Have a family member time and record the student's reading.

✔ Formative Assessment

If the student completes each task correctly, proceed to the next skill in the sequence. If not, refer to suggested Intervention 2.

Did the student...?	Intervention 2
Recall the purpose for reading?	• Explain that a "purpose" is a "reason." Explain that we pay attention to how we read the text aloud so that it sounds like we are talking. This helps us understand what we are reading. • **Say:** *We have to make sure that we are not reading too fast or too slow. We will read each word followed by the next until the words become a sentence.*
Listen attentively while teacher modeled?	• Model reading fluently while students echo- or choral-read. Conduct a cloze read as student chimes in missing words.
Read each sentence progressively?	• Guide students in reading the words, phrases and sentences by scrolling the text to expose one line at a time while it is being read.
Scroll from one line to another effortlessly?	• Have students practice tracking each word and use the return sweep with their finger as you read aloud together.
Read story with appropriate pacing?	• Practice reading the word list and match words from list to the text.
Read story with appropriate intonation?	• Select a portion of the text that requires varied intonation to practice reading. Discuss the meaning, feelings, and thoughts conveyed by the text to explain why changing the tone of voice is necessary to express meaning and understand the text.

Read Poetry with Understanding, Intonation, and Expression RF.4–5.4a

CCSS: RF.4–5.4
Read with sufficient accuracy and fluency to support comprehension.
a. Read on-level grade text with purpose and understanding.

Lesson Objectives

- Determine genre of text before reading.
- Determine purpose for reading.
- Demonstrate understanding of text that is read aloud by another (e.g., answer questions, retell story, explain what text was about).

Essential Question

How do we read a poem with expression, purpose, and understanding?

Metacognitive Strategy

Think while listening; plan, monitor, and evaluate listening; reference pictures/visuals/illustrations to predict and confirm understanding.

Academic Language

Poetry, poem, rhyming words, rhythm, pattern, intonation, expression

Additional Materials

- BLMs 1, 13, 25, 37, 49, Read for Understanding
- BLM 63, Self-Evaluation

Pre-Assess

Student's ability to listen with attention, understand what is read aloud, and use picture clues.

Introduce

- Students will be aware of a specific purpose for listening (listen to rhyming words, rhythm, intonation of voice).
- Students will demonstrate understanding by responding to wh- questions or explaining what the poem is about.
- Students will demonstrate appropriate expression and intonation as they read the poem.

State Learning Goal

Say: *Today we will read a* **poem***. The purpose for listening to the poem will be to remember what the poem is about, and to remember a word, phrase, or rhyming words we enjoyed. We will practice reading with expression and intonation, this means our voice will change as we read the words and bring them to life, so we can understand and enjoy what we read.*

Ask: *What is the purpose for listening today? (to remember what the poem is about, to listen to voice changes)*

Before Read-Aloud

Use the title to establish the theme or subject of the **poem** and to activate prior knowledge. Build background knowledge by discussing text language and key vocabulary.

Ask: *What do you* **predict** *this* **poem** *will be about? (Point out details in illustrations and key vocabulary as clues to prediction.)*

During Read-Aloud

First Read: Model reading fluently at a natural pace with **intonation, rhythm,** and **expression,** including dramatic gestures. Emphasize rhythm and **rhyming words.** Next, read the poem in a monotone, pausing inappropriately.

Ask: *Which reading did you like best? Why?*

Point out that many people think that poems are important because they are often observations written with words that rhyme and phrases that have repeating rhythms. To learn how to read a poem, we read it several times.

Second Read: Interactive reading while thinking aloud, asking thoughtful questions, and emphasizing catchy phrases and words that rhyme.

- What is this poem about?
- What ideas do you think the poet wants to communicate?
- What words rhyme?
- What are the words or phrases that catch your attention?
- How does this poem make you feel?
- What are the thoughts that come to your mind?

Third Read: Echo-read or choral-read with students emphasizing appropriate pacing, intonation, rhythm, and expression.

Say: *Lets practice reading the poem several times with rhythm and intonation. Lets use our voices to communicate what we think or what we feel when we express what the poet wrote.*

After Read-Aloud

Have students demonstrate understanding of the text by asking them to retell or explain the poem in their own words. Ask students to recall a word, phrase, or rhyming words and to explain why they enjoyed them.

Conclusion

Ask: *What did we learn today?*

We learned that when we read poems, our voices and expression change along with the words. We pay special attention to rhyming words and we read following the rhythm of the words. We read to communicate the thoughts and feelings the poet wanted to convey.

Use BLM 63 for student self-reflection, evaluation, and goal setting.

Home Connection

Ask students to take the poem home to read with a family member. Have students point out words or phrases they remember and tell family members what the poem is about.

✔ **Formative Assessment**

If the student completes each task correctly, proceed to the next skill in the sequence. If not, refer to suggested Intervention 2.

Did the student…?	Intervention 2
Recall the purpose for listening?	• Explain that a "purpose" is a "reason." Explain that we pay attention to what is read with a purpose. • **Say:** *We will listen to remember what the poem is about. We will remember words we liked and rhyming words.* (Provide examples.)
Connect to prior knowledge?	• Build new knowledge using visuals and provide personal examples that connect to what students already know.
Build understanding of vocabulary?	• Use visuals, gestures, and realia. Provide definitions and examples.
Predict what poem was about?	• Make connections between title, key vocabulary, and illustrations.
Recall rhyming words and phrases?	• Point out key rhyming words and phrases; have students echo-read them with you.
Echo- or choral-read?	• Have students clap or sway to the rhythm of poem.

Read Poetry with Accuracy, Appropriate Rate, and Expression RF.4–5.4b

CCSS: RF.4–5.4
Read with sufficient accuracy and fluency to support comprehension.
b Read on-level text orally with accuracy, appropriate rate, and expression on successive readings.

Prerequisite lesson

Fluency: Lesson 3a

Lesson Objectives

- Read with accuracy, appropriate rate, and expression.
- Distinguish into interrogative, declarative, and exclamatory sentences.
- Decode instructional-level words with increasing automaticity.
- Use phrasing techniques.

Essential Question

How do we read a poem with expression, purpose, and understanding?

Metacognitive Strategy

Use selective attention and monitor comprehension while reading.

Academic Language

Pacing, fluency, words, phrases

Additional Materials

- BLMs 2, 14, 26, 38, 50, Read for Expression
- BLM 63, Self-Evaluation

Pre-Assess

Student's ability to decode instructional-level words with automaticity, and understand text while reading it aloud.

Introduce

- Students will be aware of a specific purpose for reading.
- Students will read with proper phrasing and fluency.
- Students will demonstrate automaticity of instructional-level words.

State Learning Goal

Say: *Today we will read a* **poem**. *The purpose for reading the poem is to read with appropriate pacing and fluency. That means we will not read too fast or too slow, so that we can understand what we are reading. We will read words and phrases aloud so we can practice reading and understanding what we read.*

Ask: *What is the purpose for reading today? (I will read* **words** *and* **phrases** *aloud so I can understand what I read.)*

Before Reading

Explain that successful readers know when to pause when reading and how to read words that go together without stopping.

Say: *We are going to read the poem and practice pausing and reading words that go together naturally.*

During Reading

First Read: Teacher models reading phrases, scrolling down each line as it is read.

Second Read: Student reads each phrase progressively, scrolling down each line as they become sentences.

Third Read: Student reads the whole poem with appropriate **fluency** and **pacing**.

After Reading

Have students read to partners to demonstrate that they can use the phrasing/fluency strategy to practice pausing and reading words that go together naturally.

Conclusion

Ask: *What did we learn today?*

We learned how to pause when reading and how to read words that go together naturally. We read as we speak, not too fast and not too slow, so that we can understand what we read.

Use BLM 63 for student self-reflection, evaluation, and goal setting.

Home Connection

Ask students to take the poem home to read with a family member. Have students demonstrate the phrasing/fluency strategy to members of their family.

✔ Formative Assessment

If the student completes each task correctly, proceed to the next skill in the sequence. If not, refer to suggested Intervention 2.

Did the student…?	Intervention 2
Recall the purpose for reading?	• Explain that a "purpose" is a "reason." Explain that we pay attention to how we read the text aloud so that it sounds like we are talking. This helps us understand what we are reading. • **Say:** *We have to make sure that we are not reading too fast or too slow. We will read each word followed by the next until the words become a sentence that makes sense.*
Listen attentively while teacher modeled?	• Model reading fluently while students echo- or choral-read. Conduct a cloze read as student chimes in missing words.
Read each phrase progressively?	• Guide students in reading the words, phrases, and sentences by scrolling the text to expose one line at a time while it is being read.
Scroll from one line to another effortlessly?	• Have students practice tracking each word and use the return sweep with their finger as you read aloud together.
Read the poem with appropriate pacing?	• Guide students in clapping (swaying, marching, tapping on the table, etc.) to the rhythm of the poem as they read it together.
Read the poem with appropriate intonation?	• Orchestrate with hand gestures to mark the high and low tones of the poem. Students choral-read as teacher orchestrates.

Read Poetry to Confirm Word Recognition and Understanding

RF.4–5.4c

CCSS: RF.4–5.4
Read with sufficient accuracy and fluency to support comprehension.
c. Use context to confirm or self-correct word recognition and understanding, rereading as necessary.

Prerequisite lessons

Fluency: Lessons 3a and 3b

Lesson Objectives

- Read with purpose and understanding.
- Read with accuracy and comprehension.
- Decode instructional-level words with increasing automaticity.

Essential Questions

What do I do when I do not know what a word means?
What is an appropriate rate in reading?

Metacognitive Strategy

Use selective attention and monitor comprehension while reading.

Academic Language

Accuracy, comprehension

Additional Materials

- BLMs 3, 15, 27, 39, 51, Recognize Words
- BLM 61, Recording Time Sheet
- BLM 62, Comprehension Monitoring
- BLM 63, Self Evaluation

Pre-Assess

Student's ability to decode instructional-level words with automaticity, and understand text while reading it aloud.

Introduce

- Students will be aware of a specific purpose for reading.
- Students will read with accuracy and understanding.
- Students will demonstrate automaticity of instructional-level words.

State Learning Goal

Say: *Today we will read a* **poem**. *The purpose for reading the poem is to read with accuracy and understanding. That means we will practice reading every word correctly and understand what each word means.*

Ask: *What is the purpose for reading today? (I will read each word correctly and know what each word means.)*

Before Reading

Explain that successful readers are able to read and understand what they read. When they do not understand what they are reading, they stop and reread. They think about what they have read and determine meaning before continuing. If they cannot figure out the meaning of a word, they look for clues such as the words around the word they do not know and word parts that may provide a clue to the meaning of the word they do not know.

Say: *We are going to practice reading each word correctly, making sure we understand the meaning of each word.*

Read the list of words and have students identify words they do not know. Use context clues to explain the meaning of unknown words. Redefine words as needed. Example:

Unknown Word	Word in Context	Word Redefined
(student-generated)	as it appears in sentence	Look at word parts (structural clues). Look up in dictionary (definition). Look at surrounding words (context clues). Determine if it is a cognate.

During Reading

First Read: Teacher models reading words correctly and fluently.

Second Read: Teacher uses the Recording Time Sheet BLM (61) to monitor first fluency and accuracy rate.

Student reads each word on list. Teacher identifies and annotates student's errors and self-corrections, and discusses word/phrase relationship to overall passage (multiple meanings, synonyms/antonyms, roots, affixes).

Third Read: Student reads the whole poem aloud to self or to a partner with appropriate fluency and pacing. A second fluency and **accuracy** rate is recorded.

After Reading

Use the Comprehension Monitoring BLM (62) to monitor and record comprehension. Ask text-dependent questions to ensure student understanding. Ask students to retell or explain text in their own words to check for comprehension.

- In your own words, what is this poem about?
- Who are characters in this poem? What are their names?
- What is the setting of this poem? How do you know?
- What details in the poem tell you about the focus of the poem?
- What are they doing? How are they doing this? Why do you think they are doing this?
- What is the most interesting line in the poem? Why?
- What does the poet mean by_____? Cite evidence from the text to support your idea.
- Can this really happen? Why or why not?
- What does this poem make you think about?
- What images does this poem create in your head when you read it?
- What connections can you make to this poem?
- What is the poet's purpose in this poem?

Conclusion

Ask: *What did we learn today?*

We learned that successful readers read words correctly and understand what they read. When we read, it is important to read the words correctly and understand the meaning of the words we read.

Use BLM 63 for student self-reflection, evaluation, and goal setting.

Home Connection

Provide students a copy of the poem the Recording Time Sheet BLM. Have a family member time and record student's reading. Encourage students to ask their family members questions about the poem.

✔ Formative Assessment

If the student completes each task correctly, proceed to the next skill in the sequence. If not, refer to suggested Intervention 2.

Did the student…?	Intervention 2
Recall the purpose for reading?	• Explain that a "purpose" is a "reason." Explain that we pay attention to how we read the text aloud so that it sounds like we are talking. This helps us understand what we are reading. • **Say:** *We have to make sure that we are not reading too fast or too slow. We will read each word followed by the next until the words become a sentence that makes sense.*
Listen attentively while teacher modeled?	• Model reading fluently while students echo- or choral-read. Conduct a cloze read as student chimes in missing words.
Read each phrase progressively?	• Guide students in reading the words, phrases, and sentences by scrolling the text to expose one line at a time while it is being read.
Scroll from one line to another effortlessly?	• Have students practice tracking each word and use the return sweep with their finger as you read aloud together.
Read the poem with appropriate pacing?	• Guide students in clapping (swaying, marching, tapping on the table, etc.) to the rhythm of poem as they read the poem together.
Read the poem with appropriate intonation?	• Orchestrate with hand gestures to mark the high and low tones of the poem. Students choral-read as teacher orchestrates.

Read Drama with Understanding, Intonation, and Expression RF.4–5.4a

CCSS: RF.4–5.4
Read with sufficient accuracy and fluency to support comprehension.
a. Read on-level text with purpose and understanding.

Lesson Objectives

- Determine genre of text before reading.
- Determine purpose for reading.
- Use expression to reflect understanding and interpretation of the text.

Essential Question

How do we read a play with expression, purpose, and understanding?

Metacognitive Strategy

Think while listening/reading; plan, monitor, and interpret text; make personal connections with the text.

Academic Language

Theatre, play, acting, voice, pattern, intonation, expression, lines, dialogue, script

Additional Materials

- Pre-selected drama text (Teacher should select a drama text based on students' ages and reading levels, and on the number of students in the class).
- BLM 63, Self-Evaluation

Pre-Assess

Student's ability to listen with attention, understand what is read aloud and follow a script.

Introduce

- Students will be aware of a specific purpose for listening (listen and follow dialogue, intonation of voice).
- Students will demonstrate understanding by responding to wh- questions or explaining what the play is about.
- Students will demonstrate appropriate expression and intonation as they interpret characters.

State Learning Goal

Say: *Today we will read part of a* **play.** *The purpose for listening and reading will be to interpret or pretend to be the characters in the play.*

Explain that they will use their voices, **expressions,** and gestures to show that they understand their assigned character. They will also pay attention and follow along as other readers read their character's **lines**.

Ask: *What is the purpose for listening today? (to interpret and pretend to be different characters)*

Before Read-Aloud

Use the title and illustrations, if present, to establish the theme or subject of the play and to activate prior knowledge. Build background knowledge by discussing illustrations, text language, and key vocabulary to make certain students understand their meaning. Review the characters and have students predict by describing what each character's **voice**, actions, and personality may be like. Explain that the narrator is the person who tells or narrates parts of the story to the audience.

Ask: *What do you* **predict** *this play will be about? (Point out details in illustrations and key vocabulary as clues to prediction.)*

During Read-Aloud

First Read: Model reading fluently at natural pace with **intonation,** rhythm, and expression, including dramatic gestures. Point to each character's line in the **script** and vary the voice of each character.

Ask: *Which character did you like best? Why?*

Second Read: Interactive reading while thinking aloud, asking thoughtful questions, and emphasizing catchy phrases and body movements to convey and interpret meaning.

- What is this play about?
- What are the characters thinking and feeling?
- How do you know?
- What are the words in the play that are not **dialogue**?
- Why are they included?
- Have you ever felt, thought, or acted like any of these characters?

Third Read: Echo-read or choral-read emphasizing expression and a different voice intonation for each character.

Say: *Let's practice reading the play while giving each character a different voice. We will use our voices to interpret and reflect on what we think or what we feel when we express what the playwright wrote.*

After Read-Aloud

Have students demonstrate their understanding of the text by asking them to retell or explain the play in their own words. Motivate students to collaborate with others to practice and perform the script for the class.

Conclusion

Ask: *What did we learn today?*

We learned that when we read scripts, we use our voices and expression to pretend we are the characters in the play. We learned that a script is text that is written in dialogue, showing what each character says. The narrator reads the lines that narrate or tell the story to the audience in parts of the play.

Use BLM 63 for student self-reflection, evaluation, and goal setting.

Home Connection

Ask students to take the script home to read with a family member. Encourage students to invite members of the family to read and perform the play with them.

✔ Formative Assessment

If the student completes each task correctly, proceed to the next skill in the sequence. If not, refer to suggested Intervention 2.

Did the student…?	Intervention 2
Recall the purpose for listening?	• Explain that a "purpose" is a "reason." Explain that we pay attention to what is read for a reason. • **Say:** *We will listen to remember what the play is about, we listen to follow the script.*
Connect to prior knowledge?	• Build new knowledge using visuals and provide personal examples that connect to what students already know.
Build understanding of vocabulary?	• Use visuals, gestures, and realia. Provide definitions and examples.
Predict what play was about?	• Make connections between title, key vocabulary, and illustrations.
Read with expression?	• Have students think about the character and put themselves in his or her situation. Discuss the character's thoughts and feelings. Model acting out the words to reflect the character's thoughts, feelings, and actions.
Echo- or choral-read?	• Have student follow along tracking with their index finger as the words are read. Have students echo short lines or part of the lines. Have students chime in a key word, phrase, or expression.

Read Drama with Accuracy, Appropriate Rate, and Expression RF.4–5.4b

CCSS: RF.4–5.4
Read with sufficient accuracy and fluency to support comprehension.
b Read on-level text orally with accuracy, appropriate rate, and expression on successive readings.

Prerequisite lesson

Fluency: Lesson 4a

Lesson Objectives

- Read with accuracy, appropriate rate, and expression.
- Distinguish into interrogative, declarative, and exclamatory sentences.
- Decode instructional-level words with increasing automaticity.
- Use phrasing techniques.

Essential Questions

How does grouping words help you read better?
How do elements of the script help the reader?

Metacognitive Strategy

Use selective attention and monitor comprehension while reading.

Academic Language

Pacing, fluency, words, phrases

Additional Materials

- Pre-selected drama text (Teacher should select a drama text based on students' ages and reading levels, and on the number of students in the class).
- BLM 63, Self-Evaluation

Pre-Assess

Student's ability to decode instructional-level words with automaticity, and understand text while reading it aloud.

Introduce

- Students will be aware of a specific purpose for reading.
- Students will read with proper phrasing and fluency.
- Students will demonstrate automaticity of instructional-level words.

State Learning Goal

Say: *Today we will read part of a* **play.** *The purpose for reading is to read with appropriate pacing and fluency. That means we will not read too fast or too slow, so that we can understand what we are reading. We will read words and phrases aloud so we can practice reading and understanding what we read.*

Ask: *What is the purpose for reading today? (I will read words and phrases aloud so I can understand what I read.)*

Before Reading

Explain that successful readers know when to pause when reading and how to read words that go together without stopping.

Say: *We are going to read the play and practice pausing and reading words that go together naturally.*

During Reading

First Read: Teacher models reading phrases, scrolling down each line as it is read.

Second Read: Student reads each phrase progressively, scrolling down each line as they become sentences.

Third Read: Student reads the whole script with appropriate fluency and pacing.

After Reading

Have students read to partners to demonstrate that they can use the phrasing/fluency strategy to practice pausing and reading words that go together naturally.

Conclusion

Ask: *What did we learn today? We learned how to pause when reading and how to read words that go together naturally. We read as we speak, not too fast and not too slow, so that we can understand what we read.*

Use BLM 63 for student self-reflection, evaluation, and goal setting.

Home Connection

Ask students to take the play home to read with a family member. Have students demonstrate the phrasing/fluency strategy to their family.

✔ Formative Assessment

If the student completes each task correctly, proceed to the next skill in the sequence. If not, refer to suggested Intervention 2.

Did the student…?	Intervention 2
Recall the purpose for reading?	• Explain that a "purpose" is a "reason." Explain that we pay attention to how we read the text aloud so that it sounds like we are talking. This helps us understand what we are reading. • **Say:** *We have to make sure that we are not reading too fast or too slow. We will read each word followed by the next until the words become a sentence that makes sense.*
Listen attentively while teacher modeled?	• Model reading fluently while students echo- or choral-read. Conduct a cloze read as students chime in missing words.
Read each phrase progressively?	• Guide students in reading the words, phrases, and sentences by scrolling the text to expose one line at a time while it is being read.
Scroll from one line to another effortlessly?	• Have students practice tracking each word and use the return sweep with their finger as you read aloud together.
Read drama with appropriate pacing?	• Guide students in clapping (swaying, marching, tapping on the table, etc.) to the rhythm of the script as they read the piece together.
Read drama with appropriate intonation?	• Orchestrate with hand gestures to mark the high and low tones of the piece. Students choral-read as teacher orchestrates.

Read Drama to Confirm Word Recognition and Understanding
RF.4–5.4c

CCSS: RF.4–5.4
Read with sufficient accuracy and fluency to support comprehension.
c. Use context to confirm or self-correct word recognition and understanding, rereading as necessary.

Prerequisite lessons

Fluency: Lessons 4a and 4b

Lesson Objectives

- Read with purpose and understanding.
- Read with accuracy and comprehension.
- Decode instructional-level words with increasing automaticity.

Essential Questions

What do I do when I do not know what a word means?
What is an appropriate rate in reading?

Metacognitive Strategy

Use selective attention and monitor comprehension while reading.

Academic Language

Accuracy, comprehension

Additional Materials

- Pre-selected drama text (Teacher should select a drama text based on students' ages and reading levels, and on the number of students in the class).
- BLM 61, Recording Time Sheet
- BLM 62, Comprehension Monitoring
- BLM 63, Self Evaluation

Pre-Assess

Student's ability to decode instructional-level words with automaticity, and understand text while reading it aloud.

Introduce

- Students will be aware of a specific purpose for reading.
- Students will read with accuracy and understanding.
- Students will demonstrate automaticity of instructional-level words.

State Learning Goal

Say: *Today we will read part of a* **play***. The purpose for reading the play is to read with accuracy and understanding. That means we will practice reading every word correctly and understand what each word means.*

Ask: *What is the purpose for reading today? (I will read each word correctly and know what each word means.)*

Before Reading

Explain that successful readers are able to read and understand what they read. When they do not understand what they are reading, they stop and reread. They think about what they have read and determine meaning before continuing. If they cannot figure out the meaning of a word, they look for clues such as the words around the word they do not know and word parts that may provide a clue to the meaning of the word they do not know.

Say: *We are going to practice reading each word correctly, making sure we understand the meaning of each word.*

Teacher reads the list of words and students identify words they do not know. Using context clues, the teacher explains the meaning of unknown words. Teacher redefines words as needed. Example:

Unknown Word	Word in Context	Word Redefined
(student-generated)	As it appears in sentence	Look at word parts (structural clues). Look up in dictionary (definition). Look at surrounding words (context clues). Determine if it is a cognate.

During Reading

First Read: Teacher models reading words correctly down the list fluently.

Second Read: Teacher uses the Recording Time Sheet BLM (61) to monitor first fluency and accuracy rate.

Student reads each word on list. Teacher identifies and annotates student's errors and self-corrections, and discusses word/phrase relationship to overall passage (multiple meanings, synonyms/antonyms, roots, affixes).

Third Read: Student reads the whole play aloud to self or to a partner with appropriate fluency and pacing. A second fluency and accuracy rate is recorded.

After Reading

Use the Comprehension Monitoring BLM (62) to monitor and record comprehension. Ask text-dependent questions to ensure student understanding. Ask students to retell or explain text in their own words to check for comprehension.

- In your own words, what is this play about?
- Who are the characters in this play? What are their names?
- What is the setting of this play? How do you know?
- What are they doing? How are they doing this? Why do you think they are doing this?
- What happens during the exposition of this play?
- What events occur during the rising action?
- What is the climax? How do you know?
- What happens during the falling action?
- What is the problem and how is it resolved?
- Can this really happen? Why or why not?

Conclusion

Ask: *What did we learn today?*

We learned that successful readers read words correctly and understand what they read. When we read it is important to read the words correctly and understand the meaning of the words we read.

Use BLM 63 for student self-reflection, evaluation, and goal setting.

Home Connection

Provide the play and the recording Time Sheet BLM for students to read to family members. Have a family member time and record student's reading.

✔ Formative Assessment

If the student completes each task correctly, proceed to the next skill in the sequence. If not, refer to suggested Intervention 2.

Did the student…?	Intervention 2
Recall the purpose for reading?	• Explain that a "purpose" is a "reason." Explain that we pay attention to how we read the text aloud so that it sounds like we are talking. This helps us understand what we are reading. • **Say:** *We have to make sure that we are not reading too fast or too slow. We will read each word followed by the next until the words become a sentence that makes sense.*
Listen attentively while teacher modeled?	• Model reading fluently while students echo- or choral-read. Teacher will conduct a cloze read as student chimes in missing words.
Read each phrase progressively?	• Guide students in reading the words, phrases, and sentences by scrolling the text to expose one line at a time while it is being read.
Scroll from one line to another effortlessly?	• Have students practice tracking each word and use the return sweep with their finger as the teacher and student read aloud together.
Read the piece with appropriate pacing?	• Guide students in clapping (swaying, marching, tapping on the table, etc.) to the rhythm of the piece as they read it together.
Read the piece with appropriate intonation?	• Orchestrate with hand gestures to mark the high and low tones of the piece. Students choral-read as teacher orchestrates.

Name _____   **Date** _____

Sea Shell

by Amy Lowell

Sea Shell, Sea Shell,

    Sing me a song, O Please!

A song of ships, and sailor men,

    And parrots, and tropical trees,

Of islands lost in the Spanish Main

Which no man ever may find again,

Of fishes and corals under the waves,

And seahorses stabled in great green caves.

Sea Shell, Sea Shell,

Sing of the things you know so well.

Name _____   Date _____

Sea

Sea Shell,

Sea Shell, Sea

Sea Shell, Sea Shell,

Sing

Sing me

Sing me a

Sing me a song,

Sing me a song, O

Sing me a song, O Please!

Sea Shell

by Amy Lowell

Sea Shell, Sea Shell,

    Sing me a song, O Please!

A song of ships, and sailor men,

    And parrots, and tropical trees,

Of islands lost in the Spanish Main

Which no man ever may find again,

Of fishes and corals under the waves,

And seahorses stabled in great green caves.

Sea Shell, Sea Shell,

Sing of the things you know so well.

Name _____ **Date** _____

a

o

me

of

and

men

sea

sing

song

shell

ships

please

sailor

parrots

tropical

Sea Shell

by Amy Lowell

Sea Shell, Sea Shell,

    Sing me a song, O Please!

A song of ships, and sailor men,

    And parrots, and tropical trees,

Of islands lost in the Spanish Main

Which no man ever may find again,

Of fishes and corals under the waves,

And seahorses stabled in great green caves.

Sea Shell, Sea Shell,

Sing of the things you know so well.

Name _____ **Date** _____

Old Mr. Bear

Old Mrs. Bear was very tired.

"I need my winter sleep," she said.

Old Mr. Bear was not tired. He was very hungry. He went looking for berries. But all the other bears had eaten them.

When old Mr. Bear got home, he said, "I am hungry and tired. I need my sleep."

Old Mrs. Bear said to old Mr. Bear, "Have sweet dreams, my dear!" As Mr. Bear slept, he dreamed of eating a lot of big, sweet, juicy berries!

Name _____ **Date** _____

Old

Old Mrs.

Old Mrs. Bear

Old Mrs. Bear was

Old Mrs. Bear was very

Old Mrs. Bear was very tired.

"I

"I need

"I need my

"I need my winter

"I need my winter sleep,"

"I need my winter sleep," she

"I need my winter sleep," she said.

Old Mr. Bear

Old Mrs. Bear was very tired.

"I need my winter sleep," she said.

Old Mr. Bear was not tired. He was very hungry. He went looking for berries. But all the other bears had eaten them.

When old Mr. Bear got home, he said, "I am hungry and tired. I need my sleep."

Old Mrs. Bear said to old Mr. Bear, "Have sweet dreams, my dear!" As Mr. Bear slept, he dreamed of eating a lot of big, sweet, juicy berries!

Name _____   Date _____

all

had

old

bear

need

said

them

very

bears

eaten

other

sleep

tired

hungry

winter

berries

Old Mr. Bear

Old Mrs. Bear was very tired.

"I need my winter sleep," she said.

Old Mr. Bear was not tired. He was very hungry. He went looking for berries. But all the other bears had eaten them.

When old Mr. Bear got home, he said, "I am hungry and tired. I need my sleep."

Old Mrs. Bear said to old Mr. Bear, "Have sweet dreams, my dear!" As Mr. Bear slept, he dreamed of eating a lot of big, sweet, juicy berries!

Name _____ **Date** _____

Pluto

In 1930, Clyde William Tombaugh made an exciting discovery. He found an object in outer space. No one had observed it before. The object was named Pluto. Pluto was then added as the ninth planet in the solar system.

Today, more information about Pluto is available. Some scientists wonder if Pluto really should be counted as a planet.

In 2006, a group of astronomers met about the issue. Most of the astronomers agreed that Pluto was actually a dwarf planet. It was not one of the major planets.

Pluto is made of rocky materials, ice, and frozen gases. But the eight major planets are made of either rock or gas.

Some scientists disagree. They think Pluto should be called a major planet again.

Name _____ Date _____

In

In 1930,

In 1930, Clyde

In 1930, Clyde William

In 1930, Clyde William Tombaugh

In 1930, Clyde William Tombaugh made

In 1930, Clyde William Tombaugh made an

In 1930, Clyde William Tombaugh made an exciting

In 1930, Clyde William Tombaugh made an exciting discovery.

Pluto

In 1930, Clyde William Tombaugh made an exciting discovery. He found an object in outer space. No one had observed it before. The object was named Pluto. Pluto was then added as the ninth planet in the solar system.

Today, more information about Pluto is available. Some scientists wonder if Pluto really should be counted as a planet.

In 2006, a group of astronomers met about the issue. Most of the astronomers agreed that Pluto was actually a dwarf planet. It was not one of the major planets.

Pluto is made of rocky materials, ice, and frozen gases. But the eight major planets are made of either rock or gas.

Some scientists disagree. They think Pluto should be called a major planet again.

Name _____   **Date** _____

Clyde

found

named

ninth

outer

Pluto

solar

space

object

planet

system

exciting

observed

discovery

William Tombaugh

Pluto

In 1930, Clyde William Tombaugh made an exciting discovery. He found an object in outer space. No one had observed it before. The object was named Pluto. Pluto was then added as the ninth planet in the solar system.

Today, more information about Pluto is available. Some scientists wonder if Pluto really should be counted as a planet.

In 2006, a group of astronomers met about the issue. Most of the astronomers agreed that Pluto was actually a dwarf planet. It was not one of the major planets.

Pluto is made of rocky materials, ice, and frozen gases. But the eight major planets are made of either rock or gas.

Some scientists disagree. They think Pluto should be called a major planet again.

Name _____   Date _____

excerpted from "A Family of Squirrels"

by Arabella B. Buckley

We have a pet called Bobby. We love him very much. He is a little squirrel, living among the beech trees of the wood.

We see him every morning leaping from branch to branch. His long furry tail stretches out behind him. Sometimes he leaps right down on to the ground. He runs about and picks up beech nuts.

Sometimes he sits bolt upright on a branch, with a nut or acorn in his paws. Then his tail is bent up against his back.

We have known him for two years. When we whistle to him, he comes to us. But if anything frightens him, he darts away to the nearest tree.

Name _____ **Date** _____

We

We have

We have a

We have a pet

We have a pet called

We have a pet called Bobby.

We

We love

We love him

We love him very

We love him very much.

excerpted from "A Family of Squirrels"

by Arabella B. Buckley

We have a pet called Bobby. We love him very much. He is a little squirrel, living among the beech trees of the wood.

We see him every morning leaping from branch to branch. His long furry tail stretches out behind him. Sometimes he leaps right down on to the ground. He runs about and picks up beech nuts.

Sometimes he sits bolt upright on a branch, with a nut or acorn in his paws. Then his tail is bent up against his back.

We have known him for two years. When we whistle to him, he comes to us. But if anything frightens him, he darts away to the nearest tree.

Name _____   Date _____

pet

the

have

love

much

very

wood

among

beech

Bobby

trees

called

little

living

squirrel

excerpted from A Family of Squirrels

by Arabella B. Buckley

We have a pet called Bobby. We love him very much. He is a little squirrel, living among the beech trees of the wood.

We see him every morning leaping from branch to branch. His long furry tail stretches out behind him. Sometimes he leaps right down on to the ground. He runs about and picks up beech nuts.

Sometimes he sits bolt upright on a branch, with a nut or acorn in his paws. Then his tail is bent up against his back.

We have known him for two years. When we whistle to him, he comes to us. But if anything frightens him he darts away to the nearest tree.

Name _____ Date _____

My Shadow

by Robert Louis Stevenson

I have a little shadow that goes in and out with me,

And what can be the use of him is more than I can see.

He is very, very like me from the heels up to the head;

And I see him jump before me, when I jump into my bed.

The funniest thing about him is the way he likes to grow—

Not at all like proper children, which is always very slow;

For he sometimes shoots up taller than an India-rubber ball,

And he sometimes gets so little that there's none of him at all.

Name _____ **Date** _____

I

I have

I have a

I have a little

I have a little shadow

I have a little shadow that

I have a little shadow that goes

I have a little shadow that goes
in

I have a little shadow that goes
in and

I have a little shadow that goes
in and out

I have a little shadow that goes
in and out with

I have a little shadow that goes
in and out with me,

My Shadow

by Robert Louis Stevenson

I have a little shadow that goes
in and out with me,

And what can be the use of him
is more than I can see.

He is very, very like me from the
heels up to the head;

And I see him jump before me,
when I jump into my bed.

The funniest thing about him is
the way he likes to grow—

Not at all like proper children,
which is always very slow;

For he sometimes shoots up taller
than an India-rubber ball,

And he sometimes gets so little
that there's none of him at all.

Name _____ **Date** _____

me

and

can

him

out

see

the

use

goes

have

more

what

with

little

shadow

My Shadow

by Robert Louis Stevenson

I have a little shadow that goes in and out with me,

And what can be the use of him is more than I can see.

He is very, very like me from the heels up to the head;

And I see him jump before me, when I jump into my bed.

The funniest thing about him is the way he likes to grow—

Not at all like proper children, which is always very slow;

For he sometimes shoots up taller than an India-rubber ball,

And he sometimes gets so little that there's none of him at all.

Name _____ **Date** _____

The Park Pond

Ting's mom was a gardener at the park. One Saturday, Ting went to help her mom. In the morning, they pulled weeds. Later they went to the pond and found it full of slime and trash.

"Here are some gloves," said Ting's mom. "You can pick up the trash and put it in the trash bags. I will scoop the slime out of the water."

"Do the trash and slime make the frogs sick?" asked Ting.

"Yes, but they will be singing 'ribbet, ribbet' when the pond is clean again!"

Name _____ **Date** _____

Ting's

Ting's mom

Ting's mom was

Ting's mom was a

Ting's mom was a gardener

Ting's mom was a gardener at

Ting's mom was a gardener at the

Ting's mom was a gardener at the park.

The Park Pond

Ting's mom was a gardener at the park. One Saturday, Ting went to help her mom. In the morning, they pulled weeds. Later they went to the pond and found it full of slime and trash.

"Here are some gloves," said Ting's mom. "You can pick up the trash and put it in the trash bags. I will scoop the slime out of the water."

"Do the trash and slime make the frogs sick?" asked Ting.

"Yes, but they will be singing 'ribbet, ribbet' when the pond is clean again!"

Name _____   Date _____

a

in

to

mom

was

park

pond

Ting

slime

trash

weeds

found

later

pulled

morning

The Park Pond

Ting's mom was a gardener at the park. One Saturday, Ting went to help her mom. In the morning, they pulled weeds. Later they went to the pond and found it full of slime and trash.

"Here are some gloves," said Ting's mom. "You can pick up the trash and put it in the trash bags. I will scoop the slime out of the water."

"Do the trash and slime make the frogs sick?" asked Ting.

"Yes, but they will be singing 'ribbet, ribbet' when the pond is clean again!"

Name _____ **Date** _____

Jonas Salk

In 1952, there was a large polio epidemic. Doctors needed a way to stop the spread of the disease. Scientists thought they could stop polio with vaccines. Vaccines are injections of weakened forms of a virus.

It was hard to make a polio vaccine from a living virus. Scientists were worried about even a weakened polio virus. They feared it might still make people sick.

Dr. Jonas Salk decided to create a vaccine using dead polio viruses. Other scientists did not believe Salk's idea would work. But in 1955 he successfully made a safe vaccine. His vaccine saved thousands of lives. It helped stop the spread of polio. Salk's vaccine is the only polio vaccine now used in the United States.

Name _____ **Date** _____

In

In 1952,

In 1952 there

In 1952 there was

In 1952 there was a

In 1952 there was a large

In 1952 there was a large polio

In 1952 there was a large polio epidemic.

Jonas Salk

In 1952, there was a large polio epidemic. Doctors needed a way to stop the spread of the disease. Scientists thought they could stop polio with vaccines. Vaccines are injections of weakened forms of a virus.

It was hard to make a polio vaccine from a living virus. Scientists were worried about even a weakened polio virus. They feared it might still make people sick.

Dr. Jonas Salk decided to create a vaccine using dead polio viruses. Other scientists did not believe Salk's idea would work. But in 1955 he successfully made a safe vaccine. His vaccine saved thousands of lives. It helped stop the spread of polio. Salk's vaccine is the only polio vaccine now used in the United States.

Name _____ **Date** _____

stop

could

forms

large

polio

virus

needed

spread

disease

doctors

thought

epidemic

vaccines

weakened

injections

scientists

Jonas Salk

In 1952, there was a large polio epidemic. Doctors needed a way to stop the spread of the disease. Scientists thought they could stop polio with vaccines. Vaccines are injections of weakened forms of a virus.

It was hard to make a polio vaccine from a living virus. Scientists were worried about even a weakened polio virus. They feared it might still make people sick.

Dr. Jonas Salk decided to create a vaccine using dead polio viruses. Other scientists did not believe Salk's idea would work. But in 1955 he successfully made a safe vaccine. His vaccine saved thousands of lives. It helped stop the spread of polio. Salk's vaccine is the only polio vaccine now used in the United States.

Name _____ **Date** _____

Winston Churchill

In 1896, a young Winston Churchill joined the British army. He proved to be a fearless soldier. He wrote articles about many battles and sold them to English newspapers.

After serving in the army, Churchill was elected to Parliament. He worked for several years in the government. He was deeply respected. In 1911, he was made head of the Royal Navy.

During this time, he sent the navy on an unfortunate mission. Thousands of sailors and soldiers lost their lives on this mission. After this, Churchill was forced to resign. For a long time, he was not taken seriously.

All this changed in 1933. At that time, a new threat emerged in Europe—the rise of Nazism in Germany. Churchill rose to the challenge of rallying his country against this threat.

Name _____   **Date** _____

In

In 1896

In 1896 a

In 1896 a young

In 1896 a young Winston

In 1896 a young Winston
Churchill

In 1896 a young Winston
Churchill joined

In 1896 a young Winston
Churchill joined the

In 1896 a young Winston
Churchill joined the British

In 1896 a young Winston
Churchill joined the British
army.

Winston Churchill

In 1896, a young Winston Churchill joined the British army. He proved to be a fearless soldier. He wrote articles about many battles and sold them to English newspapers.

After serving in the army, Churchill was elected to Parliament. He worked for several years in the government. He was deeply respected. In 1911, he was made head of the Royal Navy.

During this time, he sent the navy on an unfortunate mission. Thousands of sailors and soldiers lost their lives on this mission. After this, Churchill was forced to resign. For a long time, he was not taken seriously.

All this changed in 1933. At that time, a new threat emerged in Europe—the rise of Nazism in Germany. Churchill rose to the challenge of rallying his country against this threat.

Name _____ Date _____

army

many

about

wrote

young

joined

proved

battles

British

soldier

articles

fearless

Winston Churchill

Winston Churchill

In **1896**, a young Winston Churchill joined the British army. He proved to be a fearless soldier. He wrote articles about many battles and sold them to English newspapers.

After serving in the army, Churchill was elected to Parliament. He worked for several years in the government. He was deeply respected. In **1911**, he was made head of the Royal Navy.

During this time, he sent the navy on an unfortunate mission. Thousands of sailors and soldiers lost their lives on this mission. After this, Churchill was forced to resign. For a long time, he was not taken seriously.

All this changed in **1933**. At that time, a new threat emerged in Europe—the rise of Nazism in Germany. Churchill rose to the challenge of rallying his country against this threat.

Name _____ **Date** _____

Bed in Summer

by Robert Louis Stevenson

In winter I get up at night

And dress by yellow candle-light.

In summer, quite the other way,

I have to go to bed by day.

I have to go to bed and see

The birds still hopping on the tree,

Or hear the grown-up people's feet

Still going past me in the street.

And does it not seem hard to you,

When all the sky is clear and blue,

And I should like so much to play,

to have to go to bed by day?

Name _____   Date _____

In

In winter

In winter I

In winter I get

In winter I get up

In winter I get up at

In winter I get up at night

And

And dress

And dress by

And dress by yellow

And dress by yellow candle-light.

Bed in Summer

by Robert Louis Stevenson

In winter I get up at night

And dress by yellow candle-light.

In summer, quite the other way,

I have to go to bed by day.

I have to go to bed and see

The birds still hopping on the tree,

Or hear the grown-up people's feet

Still going past me in the street.

And does it not seem hard to you,

When all the sky is clear and blue,

And I should like so much to play,

to have to go to bed by day?

Name _____   Date _____

I

at

by

bed

day

get

the

way

dress

night

other

quite

summer

winter

yellow

candle-light

Bed in Summer

by Robert Louis Stevenson

In winter I get up at night

And dress by yellow candle-light.

In summer, quite the other way,

I have to go to bed by day.

I have to go to bed and see

The birds still hopping on the tree,

Or hear the grown-up people's feet

Still going past me in the street.

And does it not seem hard to you,

When all the sky is clear and blue,

And I should like so much to play,

to have to go to bed by day?

Name _____ **Date** _____

The Car Wash

Hillside School wanted to raise money to help a school in Africa.

"We could have a spelling bee," said Connor.

"It would be better if we gave people something for the money they spend," said Mr. Lopez.

"Then let's have a car wash," said Caitlin.

"Great idea," said Mr. Lopez. "My car can be the first to be washed!"

That Saturday, Mr. Lopez's class washed more than 50 cars and made lots of money.

When Caitlin got home, her mom said, "I have some money for you, and my car's waiting in the driveway!"

"Oh no, not another car to wash!" said Caitlin.

Name _____   Date _____

Hillside School

Hillside School wanted

Hillside School wanted to

Hillside School wanted to raise

Hillside School wanted to raise
money

Hillside School wanted to raise
money to

Hillside School wanted to raise
money to help

Hillside School wanted to raise
money to help a

Hillside School wanted to raise
money to help a school

Hillside School wanted to raise
money to help a school in
Africa.

The Car Wash

Hillside School wanted to
raise money to help a school
in Africa.

"We could have a spelling
bee," said Connor.

"It would be better if we
gave people something for
the money they spend," said
Mr. Lopez.

"Then let's have a car wash,"
said Caitlin.

"Great idea," said Mr. Lopez.
"My car can be the first to be
washed!"

That Saturday, Mr. Lopez's
class washed more than 50
cars and made lots of money.

When Caitlin got home, her
mom said, "I have some
money for you, and my car's
waiting in the driveway!"

"Oh no, not another car to
wash!" said Caitlin.

Name _____ **Date** _____

a

bee

buy

for

have

said

books

could

money

raise

Africa

Connor

wanted

spelling

Hillside School

The Car Wash

Hillside School wanted to raise money to help a school in Africa.

"We could have a spelling bee," said Connor.

"It would be better if we gave people something for the money they spend," said Mr. Lopez.

"Then let's have a car wash," said Caitlin.

"Great idea," said Mr. Lopez. "My car can be the first to be washed!"

That Saturday, Mr. Lopez's class washed more than 50 cars and made lots of money.

When Caitlin got home, her mom said, "I have some money for you, and my car's waiting in the driveway!"

"Oh no, not another car to wash!" said Caitlin.

Name _____ **Date** _____

Geno's Insects

Geno spent most of his spare time looking for insects in his large backyard.

"Mom, can I bring my bug container into my room tonight, please?" asked Geno.

"The last time I let you do that, the crickets escaped and I found them throughout the house," his mother protested.

"Just one more time, and I promise that I won't let a single insect escape," pleaded Geno.

"All right, but there better not be any problems," warned his mother.

Later, Geno took out the praying mantises, and one escaped. It took Geno more than an hour to find it. Luckily, his mother and grandmother didn't notice because the praying mantis blended in with the green carpet! This was one time that camouflage saved the praying mantis' life—and Geno's, too!

Name _____ **Date** _____

Geno

Geno spent

Geno spent most

Geno spent most of

Geno spent most of his

Geno spent most of his spare

Geno spent most of his spare time

Geno spent most of his spare time looking

Geno spent most of his spare time looking for

Geno spent most of his spare time looking for insects

Geno spent most of his spare time looking for insects in

Geno spent most of his spare time looking for insects in his

Geno spent most of his spare time looking for insects in his large

Geno spent most of his spare time looking for insects in his large backyard.

Geno's Insects

Geno spent most of his spare time looking for insects in his large backyard.

"Mom, can I bring my bug container into my room tonight, please?" asked Geno.

"The last time I let you do that, the crickets escaped and I found them throughout the house," his mother protested.

"Just one more time, and I promise that I won't let a single insect escape," pleaded Geno.

"All right, but there better not be any problems," warned his mother.

Later, Geno took out the praying mantises, and one escaped. It took Geno more than an hour to find it. Luckily, his mother and grandmother didn't notice because the praying mantis blended in with the green carpet! This was one time that camouflage saved the praying mantis' life—and Geno's, too!

Name _____   **Date** _____

of

in

his

let

bug

Mom

Geno

time

spare

spent

later

bring

found

please

insects

promise

crickets

problems

protested

Geno's Insects

Geno spent most of his spare time looking for insects in his large backyard.

"Mom, can I bring my bug container into my room tonight, please?" asked Geno.

"The last time I let you do that, the crickets escaped and I found them throughout the house," his mother protested.

"Just one more time, and I promise that I won't let a single insect escape," pleaded Geno.

"All right, but there better not be any problems," warned his mother.

Later, Geno took out the praying mantises, and one escaped. It took Geno more than an hour to find it. Luckily, his mother and grandmother didn't notice because the praying mantis blended in with the green carpet! This was one time that camouflage saved the praying mantis' life—and Geno's, too!

Name _____ **Date** _____

Smiley the Crocodile

Smiley's teeth made it look like he was always smiling. But since he felt grumpy, he wanted to look grumpy.

"I am tired of smiling. I want to turn my smile into a grumpy frown," he declared. "After all, a mean crocodile can't go around wearing a happy smile."

Smiley lay awake at night wondering how to turn his happy smile into a mean frown. Finally, Smiley got an idea to flip over onto his back.

Smiley flipped over, and when he did, his smile became a frown. Everyone who saw him shook with fear, which pleased Smiley.

After a while, Smiley became very dizzy, and at that moment he decided smiling wasn't really all that bad.

Name _____   **Date** _____

Smiley's

Smiley's teeth

Smiley's teeth made

Smiley's teeth made it

Smiley's teeth made it look

Smiley's teeth made it look like

Smiley's teeth made it look like he

Smiley's teeth made it look like he was

Smiley's teeth made it look like he was always

Smiley's teeth made it look like he was always smiling.

Smiley the Crocodile

Smiley's teeth made it look like he was always smiling. But since he felt grumpy, he wanted to look grumpy.

"I am tired of smiling. I want to turn my smile into a grumpy frown," he declared. "After all, a mean crocodile can't go around wearing a happy smile."

Smiley lay awake at night wondering how to turn his happy smile into a mean frown. Finally, Smiley got an idea to flip over onto his back.

Smiley flipped over, and when he did, his smile became a frown. Everyone who saw him shook with fear, which pleased Smiley.

After a while, Smiley became very dizzy, and at that moment he decided smiling wasn't really all that bad.

Name _____ Date _____

my

but

was

felt

into

like

look

teeth

always

grumpy

wanted

Smiley's

smiling

declared

crocodile

Smiley the Crocodile

Smiley's teeth made it look like he was always smiling. But since he felt grumpy, he wanted to look grumpy.

"I am tired of smiling. I want to turn my smile into a grumpy frown," he declared. "After all, a mean crocodile can't go around wearing a happy smile."

Smiley lay awake at night wondering how to turn his happy smile into a mean frown. Finally, Smiley got an idea to flip over onto his back.

Smiley flipped over, and when he did, his smile became a frown. Everyone who saw him shook with fear, which pleased Smiley.

After a while, Smiley became very dizzy, and at that moment he decided smiling wasn't really all that bad.

Name _____ **Date** _____

an excerpt from "The Wind and the Moon"

by George Macdonald

Said the Wind to the Moon, "I will blow you out;"

You stare

In the air

Like a ghost in a chair,

Always looking what I am about—

I hate to be watched; I'll blow you out."

The Wind blew hard, and out went the Moon.

So, deep

On a heap

Of clouds to sleep,

Down lay the Wind, and slumbered soon,

Muttering low, "I've done for that Moon."

Name _____ **Date** _____

The

The Wind

The Wind blew

The Wind blew hard,

The Wind blew hard,
and

The Wind blew hard,
and out

The Wind blew hard,
and out went

The Wind blew hard,
and out went the

The Wind blew hard,
and out went the
moon.

an excerpt from
"The Wind and the Moon"

by George Macdonald

Said the Wind to the Moon, "I will blow you out;

You stare

In the air

Like a ghost in a chair,

Always looking what I am about—

I hate to be watched; I'll blow you out."

The Wind blew hard, and out went the Moon.

So, deep

On a heap

Of clouds to sleep,

Down lay the Wind, and slumbered soon,

Muttering low, "I've done for that Moon."

Name _____ **Date** _____

air

you

blow

hate

like

moon

said

what

will

wind

about

chair

ghost

stare

looking

watched

an excerpt from "The Wind and the Moon"

by George Macdonald

Said the Wind to the Moon, "I will blow you out;

You stare

In the air

Like a ghost in a chair,

Always looking what I am about—

I hate to be watched; I'll blow you out."

The Wind blew hard, and out when the Moon.

So, deep

On a heap

Of clouds to sleep,

Down lay the Wind, and slumbered soon,

Muttering low, "I've done for that Moon."

Name _____   Date _____

PJ the Parrot

Mrs. Watson had a pet bird, PJ. PJ stayed with Adam's family while Mrs. Watson went on a long vacation. Adam liked looking after PJ because he was a clever talking parrot.

PJ's talking drove everyone crazy. He talked constantly as they did their homework, ate their dinner, and watched television.

So when they went out, Adam's mom put PJ in the den and turned on the radio to a music-only station. She thought that it might stop PJ from talking so much.

But Adam's dad changed the radio to a talk-radio station, and PJ listened to a jabbering talk-show host all night long. Soon PJs favorite saying was "Hello, this is WGN talk radio."

Adam's dad and mom were eagerly counting the days to Mrs. Watson's return home.

"I hope Mrs. Watson doesn't mind that we turned PJ into a talk-show host," said Adam, laughing.

Name _____   Date _____

Mrs.

Mrs. Watson

Mrs. Watson had

Mrs. Watson had a

Mrs. Watson had a pet

Mrs. Watson had a pet
bird,

Mrs. Watson had a pet
bird, PJ.

PJ the Parrot

Mrs. Watson had a pet bird, PJ. PJ stayed with Adam's family while Mrs. Watson went on a long vacation. Adam liked looking after PJ because he was a clever talking parrot.

PJ's talking drove everyone crazy. He talked constantly as they did their homework, ate their dinner, and watched television.

So when they went out, Adam's mom put PJ in the den and turned on the radio to a music-only station. She thought that it might stop PJ from talking so much.

But Adam's dad changed the radio to a talk-radio station, and PJ listened to a jabbering talk-show host all night long. Soon PJs favorite saying was "Hello, this is WGN talk radio."

Adam's dad and mom were eagerly counting the days to Mrs. Watson's return home.

"I hope Mrs. Watson doesn't mind that we turned PJ into a talk-show host," said Adam, laughing.

Name _____   Date _____

PJ	# PJ the Parrot

PJ

pet

Adam

bird

long

liked

while

clever

family

parrot

stayed

Watson

because

looking

talking

vacation

PJ the Parrot

Mrs. Watson had a pet bird, PJ. PJ stayed with Adam's family while Mrs. Watson went on a long vacation. Adam liked looking after PJ because he was a clever talking parrot.

PJ's talking drove everyone crazy. He talked constantly as they did their homework, ate their dinner, and watched television.

So when they went out, Adam's mom put PJ in the den and turned on the radio to a music-only station. She thought that it might stop PJ from talking so much.

But Adam's dad changed the radio to a talk-radio station, and PJ listened to a jabbering talk-show host all night long. Soon PJs favorite saying was "Hello, this is WGN talk radio."

Adam's dad and mom were eagerly counting the days to Mrs. Watson's return home.

"I hope Mrs. Watson doesn't mind that we turned PJ into a talk-show host," said Adam, laughing.

Name _____ Date _____

Body Movement

Your skeleton is made up of bones. These bones do not move on their own. They need your muscles to help them move.

Have you ever volunteered for anything? If so, you know that you do it because you want to. Sometimes, it's the same with your body. For example, when you decide to pick up a pencil, kick a soccer ball, or eat a juicy apple, you have to think about it. The muscle movements are voluntary because you think about them and "tell" your muscles to move.

Some muscles, such as your heart, are involuntary muscles and move without you having to think about it.

Your muscles are connected to your brain by nerves that carry electrical signals back and forth. These nerves control when and how much your muscles should contract, or tighten. This contraction is what makes bones move.

Name _____   **Date** _____

Your

Your skeleton

Your skeleton is

Your skeleton is made

Your skeleton is made up

Your skeleton is made up of

Your skeleton is made up of bones.

These

These bones

These bones do

These bones do not

These bones do not move

These bones do not move on

These bones do not move on their

These bones do not move on their own.

Body Movement

Your skeleton is made up of bones. These bones do not move on their own. They need your muscles to help them move.

Have you ever volunteered for anything? If so, you know that you do it because you want to. Sometimes, it's the same with your body. For example, when you decide to pick up a pencil, kick a soccer ball, or eat a juicy apple, you have to think about it. The muscle movements are voluntary because you think about them and "tell" your muscles to move.

Some muscles, such as your heart, are involuntary muscles and move without you having to think about it.

Your muscles are connected to your brain by nerves that carry electrical signals back and forth. These nerves control when and how much your muscles should contract, or tighten. This contraction is what makes bones move.

Name _____   Date _____

own

help

made

move

need

kick

carry

juicy

bones

decide

soccer

muscles

signals

skeleton

voluntary

electrical

Body Movement

Your skeleton is made up of bones. These bones do not move on their own. They need your muscles to help them move.

Have you ever volunteered for anything? If so, you know that you do it because you want to. Sometimes, it's the same with your body. For example, when you decide to pick up a pencil, kick a soccer ball, or eat a juicy apple, you have to think about it. The muscle movements are voluntary because you think about them and "tell" your muscles to move.

Some muscles, such as your heart, are involuntary muscles and move without you having to think about it.

Your muscles are connected to your brain by nerves that carry electrical signals back and forth. These nerves control when and how much your muscles should contract, or tighten. This contraction is what makes bones move.

Name _____ **Date** _____

The Importance of Strong Leadership

On September 4, 1939, Winston Churchill became prime minister of Great Britain. The years Churchill had spent as a soldier and statesman helped prepare him for what would be a very trying time for his nation.

In 1940, Germany invaded France and then set its sights on Great Britain. Only a narrow sea channel separated the Nazi and English armies. Churchill's only hope was to hold the line against the powerful enemy.

Enemy submarines blocked incoming supplies and caused near starvation. Hitler's planes carried out endless air raids, destroying cities and villages throughout England and killing thousands of people. But despite many hardships, Churchill challenged his people to fight on and not surrender.

Name _____   **Date** _____

On

On September

On September 4,

On September 4, 1939,

On September 4, 1939, Winston

On September 4, 1939, Winston Churchill

On September 4, 1939, Winston Churchill became

On September 4, 1939, Winston Churchill became prime

On September 4, 1939, Winston Churchill became prime minister

On September 4, 1939, Winston Churchill became prime minister of

On September 4, 1939, Winston Churchill became prime minister of Great

On September 4, 1939, Winston Churchill became prime minister of Great Britain.

The Importance of Strong Leadership

On September 4, 1939, Winston Churchill became prime minister of Great Britain. The years Churchill had spent as a soldier and statesman helped prepare him for what would be a very trying time for his nation.

In 1940, Germany invaded France and then set its sights on Great Britain. Only a narrow sea channel separated the Nazi and English armies. Churchill's only hope was to hold the line against the powerful enemy.

Enemy submarines blocked incoming supplies and caused near starvation. Hitler's planes carried out endless air raids, destroying cities and villages throughout England and killing thousands of people. But despite many hardships, Churchill challenged his people to fight on and not surrender.

Name _____ Date _____

time

prime

spent

years

became

helped

nation

trying

prepare

soldier

minister

statesman

Great Britain

Winston Churchill

The Importance of Strong Leadership

On September 4, 1939, Winston Churchill became prime minister of Great Britain. The years Churchill had spent as a soldier and statesman helped prepare him for what would be a very trying time for his nation.

In 1940, Germany invaded France and then set its sights on Great Britain. Only a narrow sea channel separated the Nazi and English armies. Churchill's only hope was to hold the line against the powerful enemy.

Enemy submarines blocked incoming supplies and caused near starvation. Hitler's planes carried out endless air raids, destroying cities and villages throughout England and killing thousands of people. But despite many hardships, Churchill challenged his people to fight on and not surrender.

Name _____ **Date** _____

an excerpt from "The Planting of the Apple-Tree"

by William Cullen Bryant

What plant we in this apple-tree?

Buds, which the breath of summer days

Shall lengthen into leafy sprays;

Boughs where the thrush, with crimson breast,

Shall haunt and sing and hide her nest;

We plant, upon the sunny lea,

A shadow for the noontide hour,

A shelter from the summer shower,

When we plant the apple-tree.

Name _____ **Date** _____

What

What plant

What plant we

What plant we in

What plant we in this

What plant we in this apple-tree?

an excerpt from "The Planting of the Apple-Tree"

by William Cullen Bryant

What plant we in this apple-tree?

Buds, which the breath of summer days

Shall lengthen into leafy sprays;

Boughs where the thrush, with crimson breast,

Shall haunt and sing and hide her nest;

We plant, upon the sunny lea,

A shadow for the noontide hour,

A shelter from the summer shower,

When we plant the apple-tree.

Name _____ **Date** _____

buds

days

hide

nest

sing

haunt

leafy

plant

breast

boughs

breath

sprays

summer

thrush

crimson

lengthen

apple-tree

an excerpt from "The Planting of the Apple-Tree"

by William Cullen Bryant

What plant we in this apple-tree?

Buds, which the breath of summer days

Shall lengthen into leafy sprays;

Boughs where the thrush, with crimson breast,

Shall haunt and sing and hide her nest;

We plant, upon the sunny lea,

A shadow for the noontide hour,

A shelter from the summer shower,

When we plant the apple-tree.

Name _____ **Date** _____

The Dog Walkers

Dylan pulled his mother by the hand in through the doors of the animal shelter. When Dylan saw the sad animals at the animal shelter, he wanted to take each one of them home.

"Can we please take the brown dog with the brown eyes home?" pleaded Dylan to his mom.

"You know we can't have a puppy in our apartment because of the rule about no pets," said Dylan's mom.

"I have an idea for how you can help the animals in the shelter without taking any of them home," said a worker. "We are always looking for people to exercise the dogs."

"Mom, we could come every weekend and take some of the dogs out for a walk," suggested Dylan.

"That would be a good way for us to help the animals, Dylan!" said his mom.

Name _____ **Date** _____

"Can

"Can we

"Can we please

"Can we please take

"Can we please take the

"Can we please take the brown

"Can we please take the brown dog

"Can we please take the brown dog with

"Can we please take the brown dog with the

"Can we please take the brown dog with the brown

"Can we please take the brown dog with the brown eyes

"Can we please take the brown dog with the brown eyes home?"

The Dog Walkers

Dylan pulled his mother by the hand in through the doors of the animal shelter. When Dylan saw the sad animals at the animal shelter, he wanted to take each one of them home.

"Can we please take the brown dog with the brown eyes home?" pleaded Dylan to his mom.

"You know we can't have a puppy in our apartment because of the rule about no pets," said Dylan's mom.

"I have an idea for how you can help the animals in the shelter without taking any of them home," said a worker. "We are always looking for people to exercise the dogs."

"Mom, we could come every weekend and take some of the dogs out for a walk," suggested Dylan.

"That would be a good way for us to help the animals, Dylan!" said his mom.

Name _____   Date _____

sad

saw

each

hand

home

take

them

doors

Dylan

animal

mother

pulled

wanted

animals

shelter

through

The Dog Walkers

Dylan pulled his mother by the hand in through the doors of the animal shelter. When Dylan saw the sad animals at the animal shelter, he wanted to take each one of them home.

"Can we please take the brown dog with the brown eyes home?" pleaded Dylan to his mom.

"You know we can't have a puppy in our apartment because of the rule about no pets," said Dylan's mom.

"I have an idea for how you can help the animals in the shelter without taking any of them home," said a worker. "We are always looking for people to exercise the dogs."

"Mom, we could come every weekend and take some of the dogs out for a walk," suggested Dylan.

"That would be a good way for us to help the animals, Dylan!" said his mom.

Name _____ Date _____

Plant Genetics

In the mid-1800s, there was an Austrian monk and scientist named Gregor Mendel. He crossbred thousands of plants to study traits like flower color, and the texture of seed skins.

Mendel experimented to determine how parent plants pass traits to offspring. For example, when he crossed a tall plant with a short plant, he discovered that he got all tall rather than medium-sized offspring.

Mendel concluded that traits are passed on to offspring by hereditary units from each parent. One of the units is dominant. In the case of plant height, the tall-trait unit is dominant over the short-trait unit. These units came to be known as genes, and the science came to be known as genetics. Mendel is considered the "father of genetics."

Name _____   Date _____

In

In the

In the mid-1800s,

In the mid-1800s, there

In the mid-1800s, there was

In the mid-1800s, there was an

In the mid-1800s, there was an Austrian

In the mid-1800s, there was an Austrian monk

In the mid-1800s, there was an Austrian monk and

In the mid-1800s, there was an Austrian monk and

In the mid-1800s, there was an Austrian monk and scientist

In the mid-1800s, there was an Austrian monk and scientist named

In the mid-1800s, there was an Austrian monk and scientist named Gregor

In the mid-1800s, there was an Austrian monk and scientist named Gregor Mendel.

Plant Genetics

In the mid-1800s, there was an Austrian monk and scientist named Gregor Mendel. He crossbred thousands of plants to study traits like flower color, and the texture of seed skins.

Mendel experimented to determine how parent plants pass traits to offspring. For example, when he crossed a tall plant with a short plant, he discovered that he got all tall rather than medium-sized offspring.

Mendel concluded that traits are passed on to offspring by hereditary units from each parent. One of the units is dominant. In the case of plant height, the tall-trait unit is dominant over the short-trait unit. These units came to be known as genes, and the science came to be known as genetics. Mendel is considered the "father of genetics."

Name _____ **Date** _____

monk

with

named

passed

traits

Austrian

offspring

scientist

hereditary

experimented

Plant Genetics

In the mid-1800s, there was an Austrian monk and scientist named Gregor Mendel. He crossbred thousands of plants to study traits like flower color, and the texture of seed skins.

Mendel experimented to determine how parent plants pass traits to offspring. For example, when he crossed a tall plant with a short plant, he discovered that he got all tall rather than medium-sized offspring.

Mendel concluded that traits are passed on to offspring by hereditary units from each parent. One of the units is dominant. In the case of plant height, the tall-trait unit is dominant over the short-trait unit. These units came to be known as genes, and the science came to be known as genetics. Mendel is considered the "father of genetics."

Name _____ **Date** _____

Pyramids to Skyscrapers

For thousands of years, humans have erected large structures that reach high into the sky. The largest of the early structures were the pyramids. The most famous pyramids are found along the Nile River in Egypt. Of these, the largest is Khufu, known as the Great Pyramid. It consists of more than 2 million large stone blocks. The Great Pyramid stood 481 feet (160 meters) tall at the time of its completion.

The pyramids were built to protect the remains of important people, such as kings. Egyptians believed that if a dead body was preserved and protected, the soul would live on forever.

Modern-day structures called skyscrapers reach into the sky in major cities throughout the world. Instead of serving as tombs for dead bodies, skyscrapers contain stores, offices, and apartments where thousands of people shop, work, and live.

Name _____ **Date** _____

The

The largest

The largest of

The largest of the

The largest of the early

The largest of the early
structures

The largest of the early
structures were

The largest of the early
structures were the

The largest of the early
structures were the pyramids.

Pyramids to Skyscrapers

For thousands of years, humans have erected large structures that reach high into the sky. The largest of the early structures were the pyramids. The most famous pyramids are found along the Nile River in Egypt. Of these, the largest is Khufu, known as the Great Pyramid. It consists of more than 2 million large stone blocks. The Great Pyramid stood 481 feet (160 meters) tall at the time of its completion.

The pyramids were built to protect the remains of important people, such as kings. Egyptians believed that if a dead body was preserved and protected, the soul would live on forever.

Modern-day structures called skyscrapers reach into the sky in major cities throughout the world. Instead of serving as tombs for dead bodies, skyscrapers contain stores, offices, and apartments where thousands of people shop, work, and live.

Name _____   Date _____

in

of

are

for

sky

the

have

early

Egypt

found

erected

pyramids

structures

thousands

Pyramids to Skyscrapers

For thousands of years, humans have erected large structures that reach high into the sky. The largest of the early structures were the pyramids. The most famous pyramids are found along the Nile River in Egypt. Of these, the largest is Khufu, known as the Great Pyramid. It consists of more than 2 million large stone blocks. The Great Pyramid stood 481 feet (160 meters) tall at the time of its completion.

The pyramids were built to protect the remains of important people, such as kings. Egyptians believed that if a dead body was preserved and protected, the soul would live on forever.

Modern-day structures called skyscrapers reach into the sky in major cities throughout the world. Instead of serving as tombs for dead bodies, skyscrapers contain stores, offices, and apartments where thousands of people shop, work, and live.

Name _____ **Date** _____

Recording Time Sheet

Student Name: _____

Date: _____

1st Reading: _____

2nd Reading: _____

3rd Reading: _____

To calculate the student's accuracy percentage:

– Count the total number of words in the reading passage.

– Count the total number of errors.

– Subtract the number of errors from the total number of words. This is the number of words the student read correctly.

– To calculate the student's accuracy percentage, divide the number of student's correct words by the total number of words in the passage. Then multiply this number by 100.

Example:
Passage: 70 words
Student Errors: 5
Words Correct (WC): 65
Accuracy Percentage Rate: 65/70 = 92% accuracy

Comprehension Monitoring

To monitor student's comprehension of texts, ask the following questions:

For Literary Texts (fiction/poetry/drama)
- In your own words, what is this [story/poem/play] about?
- Who is/are the character(s) in this [story/poem/play]?
- Where does the [story/poem/play] take place? When does it take place?
- Are there illustrations in the [story/poem/play]? How do they help you better understand the story?
- What is/are the character(s) doing? Describe their actions.
- Is there a problem the character(s) need to solve? How do they solve it?
- How and why do the characters change over the course of the story?
- Do you think the things that happen in this [story/poem/play] are true?
- What happened at the beginning, middle, and end of the [story/poem/play]?

For Informational Texts
- What is this text about?
- Recall two important facts or details. Why are they important?
- Explain in your own words what the author is saying about _____.
- What idea does the author present first? What does the author tell us next?
- What do you think the author wants you to learn from reading this text?
- How well do you think the author conveys the information? Is the author biased?
- What photos, maps, tables, or diagrams are included? How do they help you better understand the information?
- How does _____ relate to _____?
- How does this text end/conclude?

My Fluency Self-Evaluation

Text I just read: _____

Accuracy Did I read the words correctly?	
Rate/Pace Did I read at the right speed for the text?	
Intonation and Expression Did I read with feeling and variety to engage the listeners?	
Understanding Did I read in a way that indicated that I understood the words I was reading?	

Check off one goal you want to work on.

_____ Read more accurately.

_____ Read more quickly.

_____ Read more slowly.

_____ Read with more expression.